Hudson 3 Essentials

Get Hudson 3 up and running on your system quickly
and easily

Lloyd H. Meinholz

BIRMINGHAM - MUMBAI

Hudson 3 Essentials

First published: December 2013

Production Reference: 1041213

Published by Packt Publishing Ltd.
Livery Place
35 Livery Street
Birmingham B3 2PB, UK.

ISBN 978-1-78328-055-1

www.packtpub.com

Cover Image by Abhishek Dhir (abhishekdhirimages@gmail.com)

Credits

Author
Lloyd H. Meinholz

Reviewers
Jérôme Leleu

Simone Renzo

Dan Watling

Acquisition Editors
Grant Mizen

Rebecca Youe

Lead Technical Editor
Govindan K

Technical Editors
Menza Mathew

Pratish Soman

Copy Editors
Roshni Banerjee

Sarang Chari

Tanvi Gaitonde

Mradula Hegde

Deepa Nambiar

Project Coordinator
Michelle Quadros

Proofreader
Linda Morris

Indexer
Rekha Nair

Production Coordinator
Komal Ramchandani

Cover Work
Komal Ramchandani

About the Author

Lloyd H. Meinholz is currently a senior developer and an architect at a mid-sized company, building enterprise applications. He has been building web applications using Linux, Java, and many other technologies for more than 13 years. Lloyd has mostly focused on server-side development, and often deals with topics around build and deployment. Lloyd has been programming for over 25 years.

It's hard to understand how much effort is involved in writing a book until you've done it. Completion of this book would have been impossible without the support of my family. I would like to thank Katarina, my wife, partner, and friend, for all her encouragement. I also want to thank my children, Thomas and Maria, for inspiring me.

Additionally, I would also like to thank Packt Publishing for giving me the opportunity to write this book, and for their support and guidance in the difficult task of writing this book.

About the Reviewers

Jérôme Leleu is a software architect living in Paris, France. A consultant for 7 years, he has worked in many different companies, fields, and with many different people. He has participated in many IT projects as a Developer, Technical Lead, and Projects Manager, mostly in J2EE technology. Now working in a French telecom company, he is the Software Architect of the web SSO, which supports very high traffic from millions of authentications and users every day. He is involved in open source development as the CAS (web SSO) Chairman. For more information, visit `http://www.jasig.org/cas`. Interested in security/protocol issues, he has developed several libraries, one of which is, `http://www.pac4j.org` to implement client support for protocols such as CAS, OAuth, and OpenID.

Simone Renzo is a 19-year-old student of Computer Science at the University of Milano-Bicocca, located in Milan (Italy). He is mainly skilled in advanced C and Java programming, especially on the Android and Linux side. He works as an Android Apps programmer in various companies around the world, and likes to maintain his own Android custom kernel on several devices as well. Since he was a child, he has showed a great interest towards computer studies and PC hardware. He started working on Java and Android in 2010, and since then, he has improved his skills until being noticed by many companies and communities. Now he is also working as a Redactor for a blog named ChimeraRevo.com.

I would like to thank my dad who has always supported and stimulated me to improve myself and my skills. I would also like to thank my Redaction that helped me in many ways.

Dan Watling is a professional software developer for a major education software company with over a decade of experience. He has built many projects from the ground-up using a "test-first" approach. His software is continuously integrated with Hudson from the get-go. Throughout his career, he has always focused on delivering high quality products using a variety of different technologies on various platforms. When he isn't glued to a computer, he is busy playing with his kids Edward and Luca.

I'd like to thank my wife, Gabriella, for her continued support.

www.PacktPub.com

Support files, eBooks, discount offers and more

You might want to visit www.PacktPub.com for support files and downloads related to your book.

Did you know that Packt offers eBook versions of every book published, with PDF and ePub files available? You can upgrade to the eBook version at www.PacktPub.com and as a print book customer, you are entitled to a discount on the eBook copy. Get in touch with us at service@packtpub.com for more details.

At www.PacktPub.com, you can also read a collection of free technical articles, sign up for a range of free newsletters and receive exclusive discounts and offers on Packt books and eBooks.

http://PacktLib.PacktPub.com

Do you need instant solutions to your IT questions? PacktLib is Packt's online digital book library. Here, you can access, read and search across Packt's entire library of books.

Why Subscribe?

- Fully searchable across every book published by Packt
- Copy and paste, print and bookmark content
- On demand and accessible via web browser

Free Access for Packt account holders

If you have an account with Packt at www.PacktPub.com, you can use this to access PacktLib today and view nine entirely free books. Simply use your login credentials for immediate access.

Table of Contents

Preface

Hudson 3 Essentials will provide the reader with a fast-paced and hands-on introduction to some of the many features of Hudson 3. This book will provide tools that can be used to improve the quality of software development projects. The reader will learn how to install and secure Hudson in various IT environments. This book will walk the reader through how to build, test, and deploy software.

What this book covers

Chapter 1, Why Hudson?, describes Hudson and explains how it can help many IT organizations to deliver higher quality software.

Chapter 2, Installing and Running Hudson, shows how Hudson can be installed and deployed in many different environments.

Chapter 3, Configuring and Securing Hudson, describes basic Hudson configuration and covers different methods to secure your Hudson installation.

Chapter 4, Installing and Developing Hudson Plugins, discusses several important Hudson plugins and explains how to extend the Hudson functionality by developing your own plugin.

Chapter 5, Building and Delivering with Hudson, shows how Hudson can be used to build several different types of software applications and how it can deploy a web application to an application server.

Chapter 6, Testing and Reporting with Hudson, covers how Hudson can be used to perform automated testing on software applications and generate reports describing the results.

Chapter 7, Upgrading Hudson and the Team Concept feature, goes through a basic Hudson upgrade and then demonstrates how to use the new Team Concept feature.

Appendix A, Online Resources, lists the websites for the products that were referenced in the book.

What you need for this book

All that is required to use this book is a web browser, an Internet connection, Java, and the Hudson 3 distribution.

Who this book is for

This book is for software developers who would like to automate some of the mundane work required to build and test software and improve software quality. A development manager or tester can also benefit by learning how Hudson works and gaining some visibility of test results and historical trends.

Conventions

In this book, you will find a number of styles of text that distinguish between different kinds of information. Here are some examples of these styles, and an explanation of their meaning.

Code words in text are shown as follows: "We can include other contexts through the use of the `include` directive."

A block of code is set as follows:

```
[default]
exten => s,1,Dial(Zap/1|30)
exten => s,2,Voicemail(u100)
exten => s,102,Voicemail(b100)
exten => i,1,Voicemail(s0)
```

When we wish to draw your attention to a particular part of a code block, the relevant lines or items are set in bold:

```
[default]
exten => s,1,Dial(Zap/1|30)
exten => s,2,Voicemail(u100)
exten => s,102,Voicemail(b100)
exten => i,1,Voicemail(s0)
```

Any command-line input or output is written as follows:

```
# cp /usr/src/asterisk-addons/configs/cdr_mysql.conf.sample
    /etc/asterisk/cdr_mysql.conf
```

New terms and **important words** are shown in bold. Words that you see on the screen, in menus or dialog boxes for example, appear in the text like this: "clicking the **Next** button moves you to the next screen".

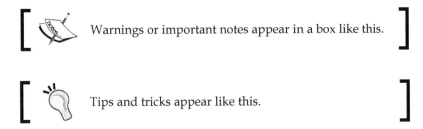

Warnings or important notes appear in a box like this.

Tips and tricks appear like this.

Reader feedback

Feedback from our readers is always welcome. Let us know what you think about this book—what you liked or may have disliked. Reader feedback is important for us to develop titles that you really get the most out of.

To send us general feedback, simply send an e-mail to feedback@packtpub.com, and mention the book title via the subject of your message. If there is a topic that you have expertise in and you are interested in either writing or contributing to a book, see our author guide on www.packtpub.com/authors.

Customer support

Now that you are the proud owner of a Packt book, we have a number of things to help you to get the most from your purchase.

Downloading the example code

You can download the example code files for all Packt books you have purchased from your account at http://www.packtpub.com. If you purchased this book elsewhere, you can visit http://www.packtpub.com/support and register to have the files e-mailed directly to you.

Errata

Although we have taken every care to ensure the accuracy of our content, mistakes do happen. If you find a mistake in one of our books—maybe a mistake in the text or the code—we would be grateful if you would report this to us. By doing so, you can save other readers from frustration and help us improve subsequent versions of this book. If you find any errata, please report them by visiting `http://www.packtpub.com/submit-errata`, selecting your book, clicking on the **errata submission form** link, and entering the details of your errata. Once your errata are verified, your submission will be accepted and the errata will be uploaded on our website, or added to any list of existing errata, under the Errata section of that title. Any existing errata can be viewed by selecting your title from `http://www.packtpub.com/support`.

Piracy

Piracy of copyright material on the Internet is an ongoing problem across all media. At Packt, we take the protection of our copyright and licenses very seriously. If you come across any illegal copies of our works, in any form, on the Internet, please provide us with the location address or website name immediately so that we can pursue a remedy.

Please contact us at copyright@packtpub.com with a link to the suspected pirated material.

We appreciate your help in protecting our authors, and our ability to bring you valuable content.

Questions

You can contact us at `questions@packtpub.com` if you are having a problem with any aspect of the book, and we will do our best to address it.

1
Why Hudson?

Hudson is an open source Java-based web application that executes and monitors jobs. These jobs are typically builds that may produce test results and/or build artifacts. Hudson is maintained as two separate projects: the Hudson core and the Hudson plugins. Hudson core is the web application with several key plugins and is maintained by core Hudson committers. Hudson plugins provide additional functionality to Hudson and are maintained by other Hudson community members.

Benefits of Hudson

Hudson can be used to improve project health and automate much of the build and deployment process. Hudson adoption can benefit multiple roles in an IT organization. It is important to note that even though Hudson is written primarily in Java, it can be used to build and test a wide variety of projects, including but not limited to: iOS apps, Android apps, JavaScript apps, and Rails applications.

Hudson can improve project health

Hudson was first designed as a continuous integration server, a fact that is still evident in the project's web address: http://hudson-ci.org. Continuous integration is one of the practices in Extreme Programming. The goal of continuous integration is to identify and resolve integration problems early in the development process instead of later, when they are more difficult to resolve. Similarly, Hudson can be used for continuous deployment, which can help identify and resolve deployment problems early in the development process. By identifying integration issues earlier in the development process, the software design can be improved and problems can be dealt with before they grow even more difficult to resolve.

Test-driven Development is another one of the practices in Extreme Programming. By ensuring that a project follows the Test-driven Development practice or, at the very least, has sufficient test coverage, Hudson can provide feedback in the form of test reports and notifications if a build or test fails.

Analysis of the project code can be accomplished using Checkstyle, PMD, FindBugs, and Sonar plugins. These plugins ensure that the project follows the defined coding conventions and detects common bugs in the application's source code. Having the project code follow common coding standards makes the code easier for new team members to understand and easier to maintain. Finding and fixing software defects is much easier and less time consuming earlier, rather than later in the development process.

Hudson can automate the build and deployment process

The build process can, over time, become very large and complicated with many steps. A common problem that can arise is that a build will work on one developer's computer, but not on another's. A Hudson job can be seen as a formalization of the build process. The Hudson job creates build artifacts at scheduled times or manually, based on the user request. Having the build process formalized forces the IT team to keep it up-to-date with any changes in the application that is being developed. This creates a build that is repeatable and portable and removes the "but it builds on my computer" problem.

Plugins for the deployment of build artifacts to an application server and publishing them to a repository are available. Using these plugins, the deployment process can also be formalized and automated. This will allow users to identify and correct deployment issues early in the development process.

IT roles in relation to Hudson

There are many roles in a typical Information Technology organization and there are four that can benefit from the adoption of Hudson: the project manager, the software developer, the tester, and the application server administrator. Depending on the size of the IT organization, these roles may span multiple departments or a single person may have more than one role. If the IT organization is large, with these roles functioning in different departments, Hudson can be the tool that brings these teams together to work toward the common goal of creating great software.

Hudson provides the project manager with a dashboard overview of the project(s) they are responsible for. They can see the build status and history, as well as view test reports and test coverage, giving them the confidence that the project is healthy and moving forward.

Getting quick feedback via the unit test reports and the build status that Hudson provides helps assure the software developer that they have not broken any existing code and that any features and/or bug fixes they are working on have not broken the build. Removing the burden of building the software for deployment allows the developer to focus on providing value to the customer by developing and improving software, instead of worrying about building and releasing the software.

The tester can benefit from using Hudson by automating some of the testing using the Selenium plugin and by viewing the test reports, which eliminates much of the mundane and repeatable part of testing. Having builds available early and often will also help the tester get a head start on developing tests and actually beginning some testing.

The application server administrator can benefit from using Hudson because continuously building and deploying the application will improve their confidence in the build process and reduce the risk of unpleasant surprises at the last minute. Hudson defines the build very clearly and this helps make the build repeatable and portable, which removes the requirement to manually build the application from the administrator.

Hudson plugins and integrations

One of the strengths of Hudson is its flexibility to extend itself using plugins. There are many useful Eclipse and community-supported plugins that extend Hudson's basic functionality. We can also extend Hudson's functionality ourselves by writing our own plugin.

Hudson integrates with many existing development, testing, and build tools commonly used by IT organizations. This integration allows developers and testers to work with the tools that they are familiar with and also to utilize the additional capabilities that Hudson provides. Some of the tools Hudson integrates with are: Git, SVN, CVS, Ant, Maven, Gradle, JUnit, TestNG, Selenium, Checkstyle, PMD, and FindBugs.

Hudson also provides a RESTful API to allow other systems access to its functionality. The API can be used for functions, such as retrieving Hudson results, triggering a new build, or creating a new job.

The Hudson back story

Hudson was created by Kohsuke Kawaguchi at Sun Microsystems as an open source continuous integration server and had its first release in February 2005. By 2008, Hudson had started to become a popular alternative to other continuous integration servers and won a Duke's Choice Award in the Developer Solutions category at Java One in May 2008.

Oracle completed the acquisition of Sun Microsystems on January 27, 2010, which included ownership of the Hudson trademark and its intellectual property. Disagreements between Oracle and Kohsuke and other project contributors over project infrastructure and trademark control began in November 2010 and ended in February 2011 with the renaming (forking) of the Hudson project to a new project named Jenkins.

Oracle and its partners have continued the development of Hudson, while Kohsuke and other project contributors continue work on the separate Jenkins project.

In May 2011, Oracle began the process of transferring the Hudson project and trademarks to the Eclipse Foundation. The Hudson project was moved to the Eclipse Foundation and became a full Eclipse project on December 12, 2012 with the release of Hudson 3.0.0.

Summary

In this chapter, we have covered what Hudson is and how it can benefit an IT organization. We have also seen how Hudson can benefit different roles in an IT organization. We've covered the history of Hudson and what types of tools it can leverage. In the next chapter, we will walk through how to install and configure Hudson, so we can begin using it to improve our software projects.

2
Installing and Running Hudson

Hudson is very easy to install and configure in a wide variety of environments. We will cover running Hudson from the `.war` file and installing Hudson into an existing application server. After we have our Hudson application running, we will see how the initial setup works and install some common plugins. Finally, we will examine the `.hudson` working directory.

We will cover four different ways to install Hudson. You can read each of the sections to compare deployment methods, or you can skip to the section that covers your preferred method of running the Hudson web application. The important thing is, that we have a working Hudson installation by the end of this chapter.

Environment variables

An environment variable is a variable that stores a value that is used by an operating system or a process (application).

In this book, I will use Unix-style environment variables in examples. If you are using Windows, simply replace `${MY_VARIABLE}` with `%MY_VARIABLE%`.

The method of setting environment variables is operating system dependent, but the format of creating and modifying environment variables is similar.

As an example, we will show how to add the JAVA_HOME environment variable on both Linux and Windows operating systems. This example assumes that the JDK has been installed to ${HOME}/jdk1.7.0_25 on Linux and to C:\jdk1.7.0_25 on Windows.

 These are not appropriate installation locations for production systems; they are just intended to be used for experimentation and prototyping.

To set the JAVA_HOME environment variable in a Linux system that uses the bash shell, add the following lines to the ${HOME}/.bashrc file:

```
export JAVA_HOME=${HOME}/jdk1.7.0_25
export PATH=${JAVA_HOME}/bin:${PATH}
```

To set the JAVA_HOME environment variable on a Windows system:

1. Right-click on **My Computer**.
2. Click on **Properties**.
3. Click on the **Advanced** tab.
4. Click on **Environment Variables**.
5. Click on **New** to add a new variable name.
6. Enter the name: JAVA_HOME.
7. Enter the value: C:\jdk1.7.0_25.
8. Select the path variable, and click on **Edit**.
9. Add %JAVA_HOME%\bin to the beginning of the value.

Setting environment variables on the Mac OS X operating system is very similar to how this is done on the Linux operating system.

Hudson prerequisites

Hudson requires a JDK (Java Development Kit). There is an official and closed source JDK that is provided by Oracle and even an open source JDK.

The Oracle JDK can be downloaded from http://www.oracle.com/technetwork/java/javase/downloads/index.html.

Instructions on how to install OpenJDK, the open source version of the JDK, can be found at http://openjdk.java.net/install/index.html.

The Oracle JDK will be used for the examples in this book, since OpenJDK installs easily only on Linux. Hudson documentation recommends using the Oracle JDK 1.6.0. However, since this version of JDK has reached its end of life (the end of public updates was on February 2013), and Hudson seems to work on JDK 1.7.0, this book will use the latest version of the 1.7.0 release, currently 1.7.0_25.

After installing the JDK, create the environment variable ${JAVA_HOME} as described previously, and set its value to the installation directory of the JDK. Then add ${JAVA_HOME}/bin to the beginning of the ${PATH} environment variable.

Additionally, it is recommended that Hudson should be run in an application server for production usage. There are application server-specific instructions on installing Hudson on the Hudson wiki http://wiki.eclipse.org/Hudson-ci/Containers.

Downloading Hudson

This book will use the latest version of Hudson (3.0.1) that is available at the time this book is written. This book will cover some of the upcoming new features of Version 3.1 in *Chapter 7, Upgrading Hudson and the Team Concept feature*. This version of Hudson can be downloaded from http://eclipse.org/downloads/download.php?file=/hudson/war/hudson-3.0.1.war.

Running Hudson WAR without an application server

The Hudson .war file includes an embedded version of the jetty servlet container. This allows the Hudson .war file to run as a standalone application.

From a console on your operating system, change the directory to the location of the Hudson .war file (hudson-3.0.1.war) and execute the following command:

```
java -jar hudson-3.0.1.war
```

It is not recommended to use this method of hosting Hudson in a production environment, but this method can be useful for quick and easy experimentation, and it will be the method used for most of the examples in this book.

The URL for Hudson using this installation method is:

```
http://localhost:8080
```

Unix/Linux installation

There are native packages for installing Hudson on different Linux distributions. These installations may be simpler and tightly integrated with the operating system (although installing and running an application server is fairly easy), but they are also less flexible and the native packages may not be up-to-date with the latest release of Hudson. For this reason, we will focus on deploying Hudson to different application servers.

Tomcat installation and setup

Tomcat is an open source application server from the Apache Software Foundation. Tomcat implements the Java Servlet and JavaServer Pages specifications, which are part of the JEE (Java Enterprise Edition) specifications, specifically the web container. The latest version of the Tomcat is 7.0.42, and it will be used for the examples in this chapter.

The Tomcat application server can be downloaded from `http://tomcat.apache.org/download-70.cgi`.

Uncompress the Tomcat file in the `${HOME}` directory on Linux systems or `C:` on Windows systems.

Set the `TOMCAT_HOME` environment variable and start Tomcat on Linux:

```
export TOMCAT_HOME=${HOME}/apache-tomcat-7.0.42
${TOMCAT_HOME}/bin/startup/sh
```

Set the `TOMCAT_HOME` environment variable and start Tomcat on Windows:

```
set TOMCAT_HOME=C:\apache-tomcat-7.0.42
%TOMCAT_HOME%\bin\startup.bat
```

Verify that Tomcat is running correctly by going to the following website:

```
http://localhost:8080/
```

You should see the following screenshot:

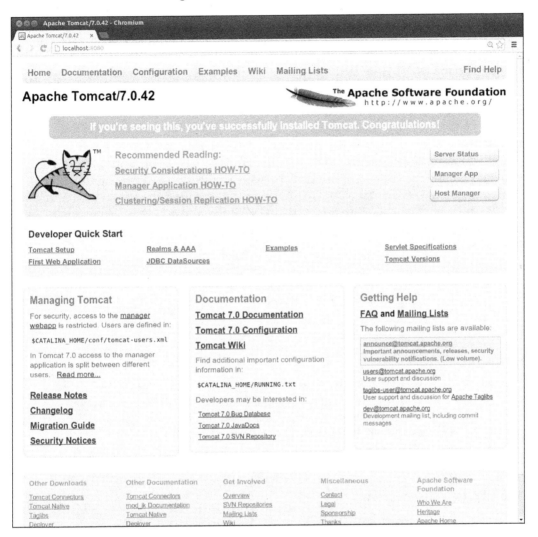

Deploying Hudson to Tomcat

Deploying the Hudson web application to Tomcat can be as easy as copying the `hudson-3.0.1.war` file to the `${TOMCAT_HOME}/webapps` directory. This uses the automatic deployment feature of Tomcat which, by default, uses part of the WAR filename to the left of `.war` as the context part of the URL. So our web address would be:

```
http://localhost:8080/hudson-3.0.1/
```

We want to get rid of the Hudson version number in the URL because this is kind of ugly. In order to change the context of the Hudson web application, we will explicitly define the context of the Hudson web application by creating the directory `${TOMCAT_HOME}/conf/Catalina/localhost` and creating the file `hudson.xml` in this directory. We will store the Hudson WAR file in the `${HOME}/hudson/` directory on Linux and the `C:\hudson` directory on Windows. The contents of the `hudson.xml` file are:

```
<Context path="/hudson"

        docBase="/home/meinholz/hudson/hudson-3.0.1.war"

        reloadable="false">

</Context>
```

Downloading the example code

You can download the example code files for all Packt books you have purchased from your account at `http://www.packtpub.com`. If you purchased this book elsewhere, you can visit `http://www.packtpub.com/support` and register to have the files e-mailed directly to you.

The URL of Hudson is now:

```
http://localhost:8080/hudson/
```

The installation and setup of Tomcat is now complete.

JBoss AS 7 installation and setup

JBoss AS (Application Server) 7 is an open source application server from RedHat. JBoss AS 7 implements the JEE 6 specifications, which include the Java Servlet and JavaServer Pages specifications, as well as other parts of the JEE6 specification. The latest community version of the JBoss AS 7 server is 7.1.1 Final, and it will be used for the examples in this chapter.

The JBoss AS 7 application server can be downloaded from
`http://www.jboss.org/jbossas/downloads`.

Decompress the JBoss AS 7 file in the `${HOME}` directory on Linux systems or
`C:` on Windows systems.

Set the `JBOSS_HOME` environment variable and create the JBoss AS 7 management
user on Linux:

```
export JBOSS_HOME=${HOME}/jboss-as-7.1.1.Final
${JBOSS_HOME}/bin/add-user.sh
```

Set the `JBOSS_HOME` environment variable, and create the JBoss AS 7 management
user on Windows:

```
set JBOSS_HOME=C:\jboss-as-7.1.1.Final%JBOSS_HOME%\bin\add-user.bat
```

For the add-user prompts, answer the following series of questions as shown in the
following screenshot:

```
● ● ● Terminal
meinholz@sandman$ $JBOSS_HOME/bin/add-user.sh

What type of user do you wish to add?
 a) Management User (mgmt-users.properties)
 b) Application User (application-users.properties)
(a):

Enter the details of the new user to add.
Realm (ManagementRealm) :
Username : admin
Password :
Re-enter Password :
The username 'admin' is easy to guess
Are you sure you want to add user 'admin' yes/no? yes
About to add user 'admin' for realm 'ManagementRealm'
Is this correct yes/no? yes
Added user 'admin' to file '/home/meinholz/jboss-as-7.1.1.Final/standalone/confi
guration/mgmt-users.properties'
Added user 'admin' to file '/home/meinholz/jboss-as-7.1.1.Final/domain/configura
tion/mgmt-users.properties'
meinholz@sandman$ █
```

Accept the default answer for the first two prompts. Select the desired account information for the username and password.

Start JBoss AS 7 on Linux:

`${JBOSS_HOME}/bin/standalone.sh`

Start JBoss AS 7 on Windows:

`%JBOSS_HOME%\bin\standalone.bat`

Verify that JBoss AS 7 is running correctly by going to the following website:

`http://localhost:8080/`

You will see the following screenshot:

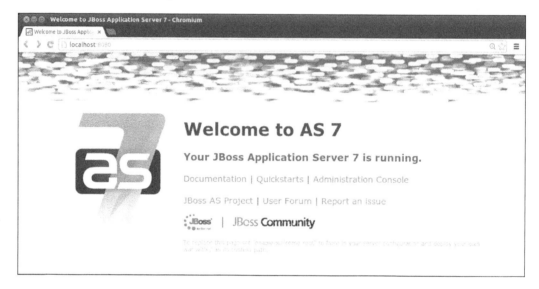

On the JBoss AS 7 welcome page, click on the **Administration Console** link.

The installation and setup of JBoss AS 7 is now complete.

Deploying Hudson to JBoss AS 7

JBoss AS 7 uses a graphical console for the deployment of web applications. On the JBoss AS 7 welcome page, click on the link to Administration Console, and provide the credentials you entered when you ran the add-user script. After you have logged in, you should be in the **Runtime** section of the server administration, and your screen should be similar to the following screenshot:

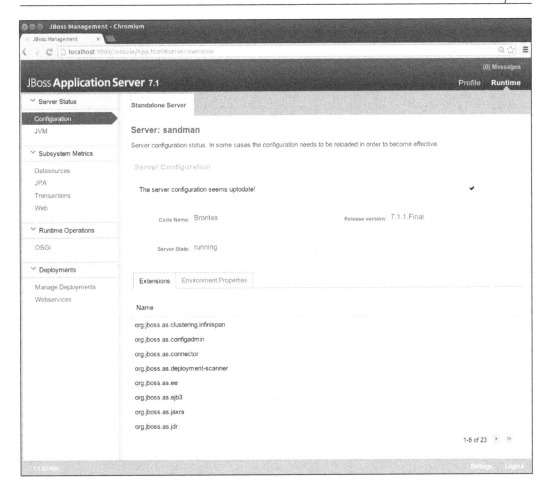

After the previous screenshot appears, follow these steps:

1. Select the **Manage Deployments** link in the left column.
2. Then click on the **Add Content** button at the top of the main pane.
3. Select the **Choose File** button, and use the file chooser to select the hudson-3.0.1.war file that you downloaded.
4. Click on the **Next** button.
5. Change **Runtime Name** from hudson-3.0.1.war to hudson.war.
6. Click on the **Save** button.

7. The **Manage Deployments** screen should now look like the following screenshot:

8. Click on the **Enable** button in the row containing **hudson-3.0.1.war** in the main pane.

9. Click on the **Confirm** button in the verification pop-up screen.

The URL of Hudson is:

```
http://localhost:8080/hudson/
```

The installation and setup of JBoss AS 7 is now complete.

GlassFish 4 installation and setup

GlassFish is an open source application server from Oracle. GlassFish 4 implements the JEE specifications, which include the Java Servlet and JavaServer Pages specifications, as well as other parts of the JEE specification. The latest version of the GlassFish 4 server is 4.0, and it will be used for the examples in this chapter.

The GlassFish 4 application server can be downloaded from `https://glassfish.java.net/download.html`.

Download the ZIP (quick start) file.

Decompress the GlassFish 4 file in the `${HOME}` directory on Linux systems or `C:` on Windows systems.

Set the `GLASSFISH_HOME` environment variable, and start GlassFish 4 on Linux:

```
export GLASSFISH_HOME=${HOME}/glassfish4
${GLASSFISH_HOME}/bin/asadmin start-domain
```

Set the `GLASSFISH_HOME` environment variable and start GlassFish 4 on Windows:

```
set GLASSFISH_HOME=C:\glassfish4%GLASSFISH_HOME%\bin\asadmin start-domain
```

Verify that GlassFish 4 is running correctly by going to the following website:

```
http://localhost:8080/
```

You will see the following screenshot:

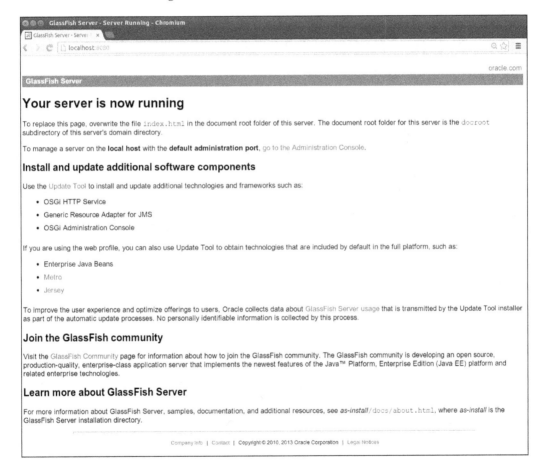

Modifying GlassFish 4 settings

There is an issue with GlassFish 4 CDI detection that causes the deployment of Hudson 3.0.1 to fail. This issue is discussed in the following forum entry:

```
http://www.eclipse.org/forums/index.php/t/490794/
```

The workaround suggested is to enter the following command:

```
${GLASSFISH_HOME}/bin/asadmin set configs.config.server-config.
cdi-service.enable-implicit-cdi=false
```

This will allow the Hudson 3.0.1 WAR file to be deployed to the GlassFish 4 application server.

Deploying Hudson to GlassFish 4

To deploy Hudson to GlassFish 4, follow these steps;

1. From the Hudson welcome page, click on the **Administration Console** link. The GlassFish 4 Administration Console should look like the following screenshot:

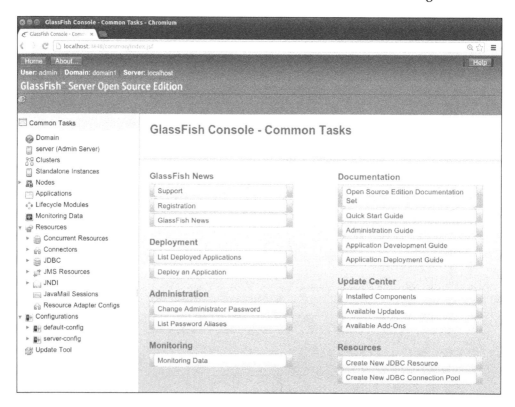

---

2. In the center pane of the screen, click on the **Deploy an Application** button.

3. Click on the **Choose File** button, and use the file chooser to select the `hudson-3.0.1.war` file that you downloaded.

4. Change the **Context Root** from `hudson-3.0.1` to `hudson`.

The GlassFish 4 Administration Console should look like the following screenshot:

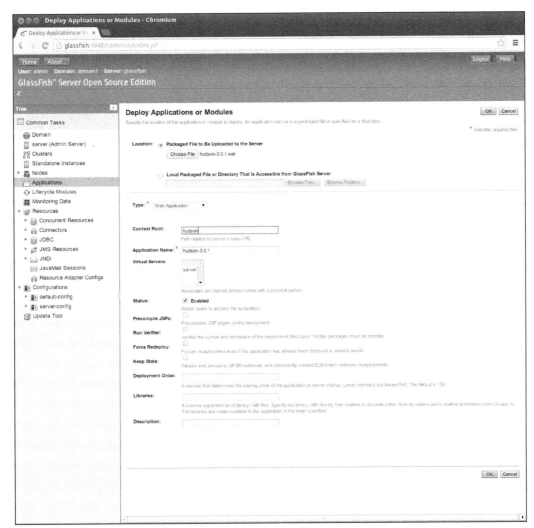

The URL of Hudson is as follows:

`http://localhost:8080/hudson/`

The installation and setup of GlassFish 4 is now complete.

Hudson CI Server initial setup

We have seen how Hudson can be run as a standalone application or deployed to common application servers. The examples will continue by running Hudson as a standalone application.

Having started the Hudson application as a standalone application, as described previously, we can now open a web browser and enter the following address in the URL:

```
http://localhost:8080/
```

The Hudson web application needs some initial setup. The first screen that you will see should be similar to the following screenshot:

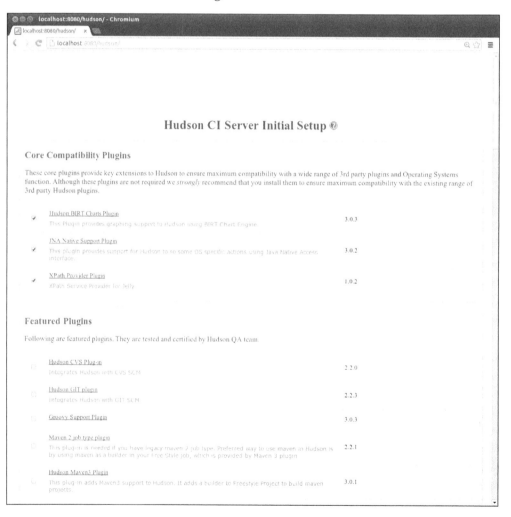

For now, we won't select any plugins except **Core Compatibility Plugins** that are selected by default. Click on the **Finish** button at the bottom of the page. It will take a few minutes for Hudson to complete configuring itself. Once the initial configuration is complete, you should see the following screenshot:

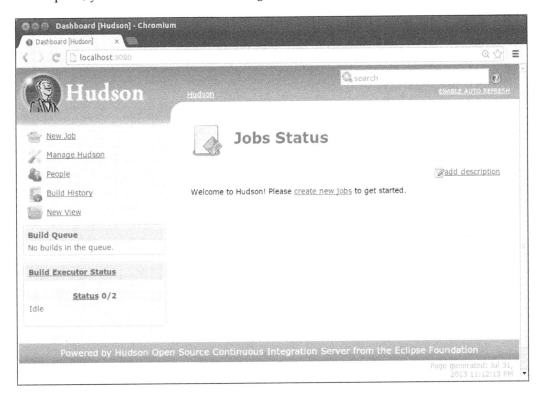

Congratulations! Hudson is ready to go.

Hudson Home directory

By default, the Hudson Home directory is ${HOME}/.hudson. It is possible to change the location of the Hudson Home directory by setting the HUDSON_HOME environment variable before starting the application server, or by setting the HUDSON_HOME system property or JNDI environment variable in your application server. For application server-specific documentation refer to:

http://wiki.eclipse.org/Containers

The most interesting item in the .hudson directory is the jobs directory. This will be the location of all the jobs that we will define during the course of this book.

 The Hudson Home directory will be created in the ${HOME} directory of the user running the web application. Since Hudson can run scripts, it is more secure if the application server that is running Hudson is not running as the root or as an administrator user. This will prevent a malicious or careless user from running destructive scripts.

Summary

In this chapter, we've run Hudson as a standalone application from the WAR file and shown how to deploy Hudson to three popular open source application servers, namely, Apache Tomcat, JBoss AS, and Glassfish. We have also seen where Hudson stores its configuration settings and job information. In the next chapter, we will configure and secure our Hudson 3 server.

3
Configuring and Securing Hudson

Now that we have Hudson installed and the initial configuration completed, we will begin with the basic configuration tasks. Later in this chapter, we will discuss many options that are available to secure your Hudson instance. Finally, we will cover what customizations are available.

Hudson home page

If you are running Hudson from the `.war` file, the Hudson home page is located at `http://localhost:8080/`.

If you are running Hudson in an application server and followed the instructions from *Chapter 2, Installing and Running Hudson*, the Hudson home page is located at `http://localhost:8080/hudson/`.

The examples in this book will assume you are running Hudson from the `.war` file.

Hudson help

The wiki for the Hudson CI server is located at `http://wiki.eclipse.org/Hudson-ci`.

Also, many pages in the Hudson web application have the following icon, which is a blue circle with a question mark in it:

Clicking on the preceding icon will expand a hidden text box that contains contextual help, and clicking on the icon again will hide the text box.

Configuring Hudson

Hudson configuration is accessible via the **Manage Hudson** link on the menu on the left side of Hudson's home page. The **Manage Hudson** page should look similar to the following screenshot:

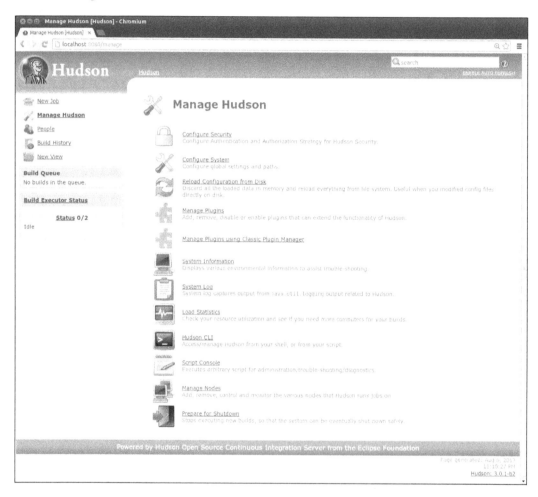

Configuring the system

On the **Manage Hudson** page, click on the **Configure System** link in the main panel of the page. This will bring you to the **System Configurations** page, shown as follows:

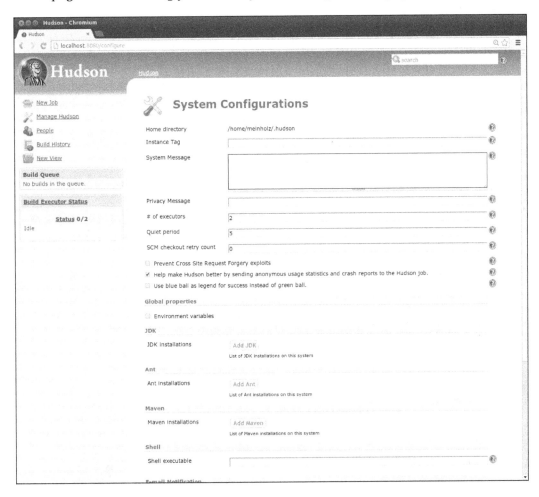

We will not change the settings in the top half of the page. You can view the online help for any of the settings to determine if you want to change them. Once your Hudson installation is being used more heavily, the settings for **# of executors** and **Quiet period** should be reviewed, as these may have an impact on your system's performance.

Configuring JDK

Java is commonly used in Hudson jobs. **Java Development Kit** (**JDK**) is required to compile the Java applications. We will configure JDK so that it can be used to execute Hudson jobs.

Because of the licensing restrictions of Oracle JDK, we are not able to automatically install JDK for Hudson to use its builds. Luckily in *Chapter 2*, *Installing and Running Hudson*, we downloaded Oracle JDK and installed it. To add JDK, click on the **Add JDK** button in the **JDK** section in the main panel. Deselect the **Install automatically** checkbox. Enter Oracle JDK 1.7.0_25 in the **JDK name** field, and the directory containing the JDK we installed in *Chapter 2*, *Installing and Running Hudson* in the **JAVA_HOME** field. The JDK installation section is shown in the following screenshot:

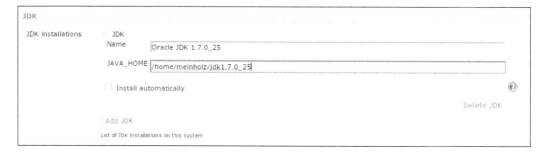

In case your jobs have different JDK requirements, multiple JDK configurations can be defined as shown in the preceding screenshot.

Configuring Ant

Ant is a commonly used build tool in the Java community, so we will configure it so that it is available for any future projects that we want to build. We are already on the **System Configurations** page. In the main panel find the **Ant** section and click on the **Add Ant** button. Leave the **Install automatically** checkbox selected. This will download Ant from an Apache Software Foundation server and install it automatically. The latest version of Ant that is offered by this release of Hudson is **Ant version 1.8.2**. A name must be provided for this Ant installation, so enter Ant 1.8.2 in the **Ant Name** textbox. The **Ant Installations** section is shown in the following screenshot:

Finally, click on the **Save** button provided at the bottom of the page.

Ant 1.8.2 should be sufficient for most Ant projects, but if there is a requirement for a specific version of Ant that isn't offered in the **Version** drop-down list, you can always download the version of Ant that you need from http://ant.apache.org/, install it yourself, and configure it similar to the way we configured JDK.

As with the JDK configuration, if your jobs require different versions of Ant, multiple Ant configurations can be defined as shown in the preceding screenshot.

Configuring Maven

Maven is a commonly used build tool in the Java community, so we will configure it so that it is available for any future projects that we want to build. On the **System Configurations** page, in the main panel find the **Maven** section and click on the **Add Maven** button. Leave the **Install automatically** checkbox selected. This will download Maven from an Apache Software Foundation server and install it automatically. The latest version of Maven that is offered by this release of Hudson is **Maven version 3.0.4**. A name must be provided for this Maven installation, so enter Maven 3.0.4 in the **Maven Name** textbox. The **Maven Installations** section is shown in the following screenshot:

Finally, click on the **Save** button provided at the bottom of the page.

Maven 3.0.4 should be sufficient for most Maven projects, but if there is a requirement for a specific version of Maven that isn't offered in the **Version** drop-down list, you can always download the version of Maven that you need from `http://maven.apache.org/`, install it yourself, and configure it similar to the way we configured JDK.

As with the JDK configuration, if your jobs require different versions of Maven, multiple Maven configurations can be defined as described in the preceding screenshot.

Configuring Hudson for sending e-mails

Hudson can be configured to send e-mails to users when certain events occur. To configure the ability to send e-mails, Hudson must be able to access an SMTP server. This information can be provided by a system administrator. These settings are at the bottom of the **System Configurations** page. In the **E-mail Notification** section, click on the **Advanced** setting. Many SMTP servers require authentication to protect them from being used to send spam. If SMTP authentication is required, check the box next to the **Use SMTP Authentication** option. The SMTP settings are as shown in the following screenshot:

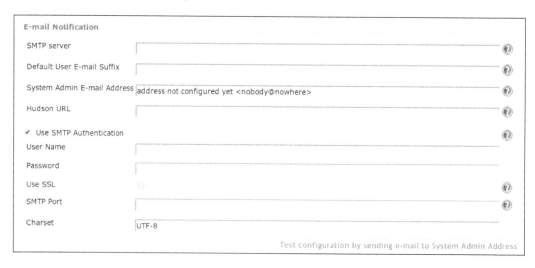

After entering the **SMTP server** information, validate the SMTP setting by clicking on the **Test configuration by sending e-mail to System Admin Address** button at the bottom of the page.

Backing up Hudson

It is very easy to make a mistake configuring Hudson security and lock yourself out of the application. Since we have just completed the initial configuration, now would be a good time to back up the Hudson configuration. We will manually back up Hudson for now, but in *Chapter 4, Installing and Developing Hudson Plugins*, we will discuss a plugin that can automate backups and provide a cleaner solution. Hudson configuration is stored in ${HOME}/.hudson or in the ${HUDSON_HOME} location provided as an alternative. We will copy the .hudson directory into a newly created backup directory.

```
mkdir ${HOME}/backup
cp -R ${HOME}/.hudson ${HOME}/backup/00000000000.
```

Configuring security

The default Hudson installation has no security enabled. This may be acceptable for a test server on a home network or for a small team on a computer that isn't accessible from the Internet, but may not be acceptable for larger installations.

On the **Manage Hudson** page, click on the **Configure Security** link. This will bring you to the **Configure Security** page. Select the **Enable security** checkbox and you should see the following screenshot:

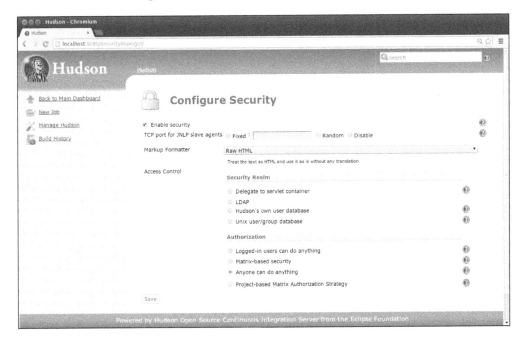

There are two aspects to access control: **authentication** and **authorization**. Authentication is a method of identifying a user. Authorization controls which action an authenticated user can perform.

Hudson authentication

Hudson supports four methods for authentication, and they are as follows:

- **Delegate to servlet container**:

  This authentication method will use the users and groups that are defined in the application server. This approach is dependent on the application server. This method is not an option when running Hudson as a standalone application.

- **LDAP**:

  This authentication method will use an **LDAP (Lightweight Directory Authentication Protocol)** server. This method is useful if an LDAP server is already available and used for authenticating other services. The settings for connecting to the LDAP server should be provided by the LDAP administrator. Clicking on the **LDAP** radio button and then the **Advanced...** button will display the full LDAP configuration parameters.

- **Hudson's own user database**:

  This authentication method uses Hudson's internal user database. This option allows the users to sign themselves up and receive an e-mail notification of the account creation.

- **UNIX user/group database**:

  This authentication method is only available on a UNIX-style operating system. Hudson will access the UNIX user/group database using **PAM** (**Pluggable Authentication Modules**). The user running Hudson must be a member of the shadow group and have access to PAM.

Hudson authorization

Hudson supports four methods for authorization, and they are as follows:

- **Logged-in users can do anything**:

  This authorization method allows authenticated users to perform any Hudson action. Anonymous (unauthenticated) users have a read-only access to Hudson.

- **Matrix-based security**:

  This authorization method uses a table to assign permissions to a user or group (depending on the authentication method). Each row represents a user or group and each column represents permission.

- **Anyone can do anything**:

  This authorization method allows authenticated and anonymous (unauthenticated) users to perform any Hudson action.

- **Project-based Matrix Authorization Strategy**:

  This authorization method is an extension of **Matrix-based security**, but the permissions matrix can be defined for each job instead of defining it for the entire site. This is accomplished on the job configuration screen.

Defining a simple security policy

We will define a simple policy for our Hudson instance. We will use Hudson's internal user database for authentication and Matrix-based security for authorization.

On the **Manage Hudson** page, click on the **Configure Security** link. This will bring you to the **System Configurations** page. Select the **Enable security** checkbox.

In the **Security Realm** section, choose the **Hudson's own user database** radio button. The screenshot should look as follows:

At the bottom of the page, click on the **Save** button. This change results in the addition of the **Manage Users** link on the **Manage Hudson** page; click on the link. Click on the **Create User** link on the left-hand side of the screen. Create an admin user with the following settings:

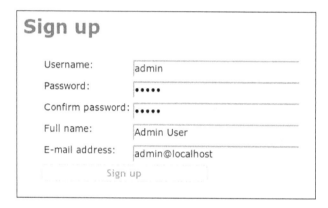

Click on the login link on the upper-right side of the page and log in as the admin user that we just created.

Click on the **Configure Security** link on the **Manage Hudson** page. In the **Authorization** section, select the **Matrix-based security** radio button. In the **User/ Group** section to add textbox, type admin and click on the **Add** button. Give the admin user all permissions and only **Read** permissions to the **Anonymous** user. The screenshot is shown as follows:

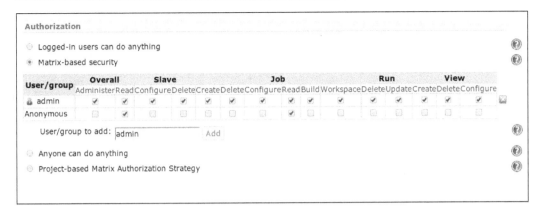

At the bottom of the page, click on the **Save** button.

Validate the settings by logging out of Hudson and verifying that you have read-only privileges. Then, log back in to Hudson as the admin user and verify that you have full privileges to Hudson.

Summary

We have configured the Hudson system and security settings in this chapter. We have specified the JDK, Ant, and Maven installations, which will be used for building projects. We have also configured SMTP settings to enable e-mail notifications. Finally, we have covered the options for authentication and authorization and configured basic security using Hudson's built-in user database, and created a Matrix-based security policy for our Hudson installation. In the next chapter, we will install Hudson plugins and cover how we can add custom functionality to Hudson by writing our own plugins.

4
Installing and Developing Hudson Plugins

This chapter will describe the Hudson plugin system, the common Hudson plugins, and how to implement a customized plugin.

What is a plugin?

A plugin is a software component that extends the functionality of a software application, in our case it's Hudson. Hudson was designed to be easily extended by creating and installing plugins. While Hudson itself forms the basis for a robust job scheduling tool, it is the plugin's architecture and the plugins themselves that give Hudson much of its flexibility and usefulness.

Installing plugins

A Hudson plugin may be installed via the Internet or via a **Hudson Plugin Interface (HPI)** file.

On the Hudson home page, click on the **Manage Hudson** link. On the **Manage Hudson** page, click on the **Manage Plugins** link. This will bring you to the **Hudson Plugin Manager** page, which is shown in the following screenshot:

Hudson Plugin Manager

Updates	Available	Installed	Advanced

Updates are available for the following plugin. Select the plugins and click update to download and update the plugins. Hudson restart required after update.

All plugins are up to date.

There are four tabs on the **Hudson Plugin Manager** page:

- **Updates**: This tab will contain those installed plugins that have updates available.

- **Available**: This tab has five sections, namely, **Compatibility**, **Featured**, **Recommended**, **Others**, and **Search**.

  Plugins in the **Compatibility** section are recommended to ensure that Hudson works well with the other plugins.

  Plugins in the **Featured** section are developed and maintained by the Hudson core team, and they are tested and certified by the Hudson QA team.

  Plugins in the **Recommended** section are actively maintained by the Hudson community developers, and they are tested and certified by the Hudson QA team.

  Plugins in the **Others** section are provided by other Hudson Community developers. These plugins are not tested and certified by the Hudson QA team, but they are tested to load correctly in Hudson.

  The **Search** tab allows searching for a plugin, using a specified search string.

- **Installed**: This tab displays all the plugins that are installed. The version number of the plugin is displayed along with a **Disable** button. When updates to the plugin are installed, there is also a button to downgrade the plugin version.

- **Advanced**: This tab allows you to configure a proxy server if your network requires it. You can also perform a manual installation of the plugin by uploading a plugin file (the `.hpi` file). You are also able to configure a different update site and to refresh the updates.

As a plugin is installed, it will be downloaded from the Hudson 3 update center. After the plugin is installed, Hudson needs to be restarted before the plugin can be used. If Hudson is being run in an application server, then we'll have a way to reload the Hudson application. If Hudson is being run as a standalone application, the server should be restarted.

You can verify the plugin has been installed by looking in the **Installed** tab of the **Hudson Plugin Manager** page and by looking in the `${HUDSON_HOME}/plugins` directory.

When you choose a plugin to install, the plugin may have dependencies on other plugins. The selected plugin as well as all the dependent plugins will be installed. Also, some plugins are a collection of other plugins.

Installing featured plugins

We begin by clicking on the **Featured** link on the **Available** tab of the **Hudson Plugin Manager** page. The page is shown in the following screenshot:

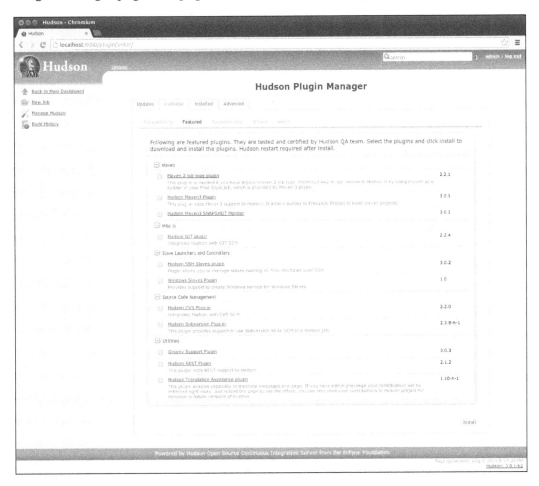

Click the checkbox next to the following three plugins:

- **Hudson Maven3 Plugin**: It adds the Maven 3 build step to Hudson free-style software jobs.

- **Hudson GIT plugin**: It allows Hudson to use GIT as a build **Source Code Managements** server.

- **Groovy Support Plugin**: It adds the ability for Hudson to directly execute the Groovy code.

Click on the **Install** button at the bottom of the page.

It may take some time for Hudson to download and install the plugins. A green checkmark will appear next to each plugin after it has been successfully installed. These plugins will be used in *Chapter 5, Building and Delivering with Hudson*.

Installing recommended plugins

We begin by clicking on the **Recommended** link on the **Available** tab of the **Hudson Plugin Manager** page. Then, click on the checkbox next to the following five plugins:

- **Static Analysis Collector Plugin**: It collects the results of the analysis by other plugins (**Checkstyle**, **DRY**, **FindBugs**, **PMD**, **Tasks** and **Warnings**) and shows the combined results in a trend graph.

- **Checkstyle Plugin**: It generates trend reports for **Checkstyle**, an open source static code analysis program that checks if source code follows specified coding rules.

- **DRY Plugin**: It generates reports of a duplicated source code in a project.

- **FindBugs Plugin**: It generates trend reports for **FindBugs**, an open source tool that uses static code analysis to look for bugs in the source code.

- **PMD Plugin**: It generates trend reports for **PMD**, an open source static code analysis program that looks for common programming flaws.

Then, click on the **Install** button at the bottom of the page. These plugins will be used in *Chapter 6, Testing and Reporting with Hudson*.

Installing other plugins

We begin by clicking on the **Others** link on the **Available** tab of the **Hudson Plugin Manager page**. Then, click on the checkbox next to the following three plugins, which will be used in the next two chapters:

- **Github Plugin**: It integrates Hudson jobs with the Github projects. Github is a popular web-based hosting service for software development projects that use Git.

- **Hudson Groovy builder Plugin**: It adds an Execute Groovy script and Execute system Groovy script as a build step. The groovy script can be run inside Hudson's JVM to have access to Hudson's internal or external data.

- **ThinBackup Plugin**: It will backup global and job specific configurations and includes the ability to schedule a backup or initial a backup ad hoc.

Then, click on the **Install** button at the bottom of the page.

Plugin configuration

We will configure most of the plugins we have just installed in *Chapter 5, Building and Delivering with Hudson* and *Chapter 6, Testing and Reporting with Hudson*. We will now use the **ThinBackup** plugin that we have just installed to back up our Hudson configuration.

The ThinBackup plugin

We will use the **ThinBackup** plugin to schedule a backup of our Hudson configuration. From the Hudson home page, click on the **Manage Hudson** link. On the **Manage Hudson** page, you will notice there is a new **ThinBackup** link towards the end of the page; click on it. The **ThinBackup** page is shown in the following screenshot:

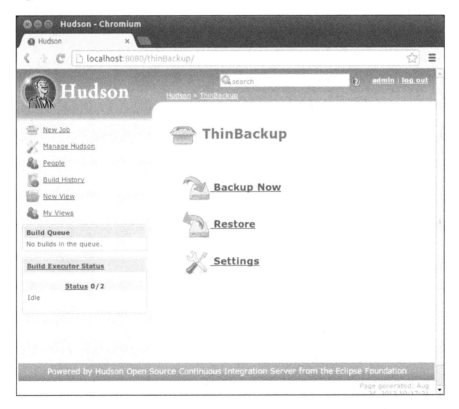

The **ThinBackup** page contains three options: **Backup Now**, **Restore**, and **Settings**. Click on the **Settings** link.

The **ThinBackup** plugin has two types of backups: **full backups** and **differential backups**. A full backup will back up everything that has been described in the **thinBackup Configuration** page. A differential backup will back up only files whose modification is done after the last full backup was performed.

A **backup set** is a full backup and the differential backups that reference it.

Configuring our backup strategy

The backup's strategy will be as follows:

- Backups will be stored in the ${HOME }/hudson/backups directory. This could be on a different file system than the ${HUDSON_HOME} directory.

- Create a full backup every Sunday night at 11 p.m.

- Create a differential backup every Monday through Saturday night at 11 p.m.

- Keep four weeks of backups.

Environment variables may be used when specifying the **Backup directory** value in the **thinBackup Configuration** page. The environment variable should be in the following format: ${ENVIRONMENT_VARIABLE}.

ThinBackup uses the **crontab** format for scheduling. Cron is a UNIX utility for scheduling jobs. The crontab format contains five fields, each separated by a space. The fields are given as follows:

- minute (0 - 59)

- hour (0 - 23)

- day of month (1 - 31)

- month (1 - 12)

- day of week (0 - 6 are Sunday to Saturday)

"Every Sunday at 11 p.m." would be represented in the crontab notation as:

0 22 * * 0

"Every Monday through Saturday night at 11 p.m." would be represented in the crontab notation like this:

0 22 * * 1-6

More details of the crontab notation can be found on the Wikipedia page at `http://en.wikipedia.org/wiki/Cron`

There are other settings for the **ThinBackup** plugin that are explained by clicking on the question mark icon to the right of the option. After implementing the preceding backup strategy, the **thinBackup Configuration** page is shown in the following screenshot:

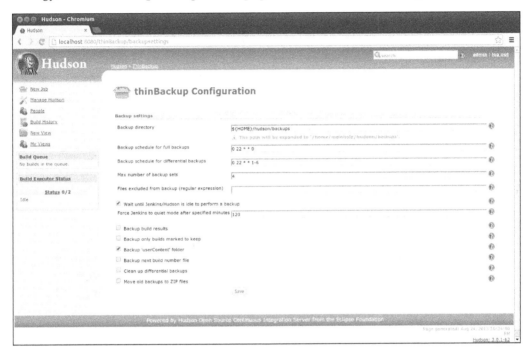

Creating a Hudson plugin

In this section, we will create a sample Hudson plugin. In order to create a Hudson plugin, we will use the **Apache Maven** project. Maven is a build tool that is commonly used by Java projects. This example will use Maven Version 3.1.0, which was the latest available version when this book was being written. Other versions of Maven should also work.

Hudson uses Jelly for creating views. Jelly is an XML-based scripting and processing engine. To find out more about Jelly, the project page is located at `http://commons.apache.org/proper/commons-jelly/`.

You do not need to download or install Jelly, but understanding how Jelly works will be necessary when writing more sophisticated plugins.

Downloading and installing Apache Maven

The Apache Maven distribution can be downloaded at `http://maven.apache.org/download.cgi`. Download the distribution that is appropriate for your platform, set the `MAVEN_HOME` environment variable, and append `${MAVEN_HOME}/bin` (or `%MAVEN_HOME%\bin`) to the `${PATH}` environment variable. Confirm that Maven is installed correctly by typing the following command:

```
mvn -version
```

The output should look as follows:

```
Apache Maven 3.1.0 (893ca28a1da9d5f51ac03827af98bb730128f9f2; 2013-06-27
22:15:32-0400)

Maven home: /usr/local/apache/maven

Java version: 1.6.0_45, vendor: Sun Microsystems Inc.

Java home: /home/meinholz/jdk1..0_5/jre

Default locale: en_US, platform encoding: UTF-8

OS name: "linux", version: "3.8.0-29-generic", arch: "amd64",
family: "unix"
```

Adding the Maven HPI plugin

There is an Apache Maven plugin to aid in the development of Hudson plugins. To make this plugin available to Maven, create the `${HOME}/.m2` directory if one does not exists. In this directory, create a file named `settings.xml` and add the following contents:

```xml
<?xml version="1.0"?>
<settings xsi:schemaLocation="http://maven.apache.org/SETTINGS/1.1.0
                    http://maven.apache.org/xsd/settings-1.1.0.xsd"
  xmlns="http://maven.apache.org/SETTINGS/1.1.0"
  xmlns:xsi="http://www.w3.org/2001/XMLSchema-instance">
  <pluginGroups>
    <pluginGroup>org.eclipse.hudson.tools</pluginGroup>
  </pluginGroups>
</settings>
```

The `pluginGroups` sections should be added if there is an existing `settings.xml` file.

Using JDK 1.6

There is a bug with the version of the Maven HPI plugin that is included with Hudson 3.0. This bug prevents the Maven HPI plugin from working with JDK 1.7. The Hudson 3.1 release has fixed this bug. In order to work through the following example, download and install JDK 1.6 as we did in *Chapter 2, Installing and Running Hudson*. Remember to set the JAVA_HOME and PATH environment variables.

Creating the sample-plugin project

For creating the **sample-plugin** project, enter the following command:

```
mvn hpi:create
```

This command will download the software needed to support the HPI plugin development, which may take a while. The command will also prompt the user for the Maven groupId and package. Enter the following values:

```
Enter the groupId of your plugin: org.sample.hudson
Enter the artifactId of your plugin: sample-plugin
```

This will create the sample-plugin directory that contains the skeleton of a Hudson plugin project.

Structure of the sample-plugin project

The directory structure of the sample-plugin project will be very familiar for those who have worked in Maven projects.

- pom.xml: This is the Maven **POM** (**Project Object Model**) file that represents the project
- src/main/java: This is the directory containing Java source files
- src/main/resources: This is the directory containing Jelly view files
- src/main/webapp: This is the directory containing static web resources (HTML, images, and so on.)

There should be a java file in the src/main/java directory, several jelly files in the src/main/resources directory, and an HTML file in the src/main/webapp directory.

Creating the sample-plugin HPI file

The HPI file can be generated with the following command:

```
mvn package
```

The HPI file can be found at sample-plugin/target/sample-plugin.hpi.

Running the sample-plugin project

The HPI Maven plugin provides an embedded version of the jetty server that can run Hudson and `sample-plugin`. This can be accomplished with the following command:

`mvn hpi:run`

The Hudson application with `sample-plugin` should be available at `http://localhost:8080`.

First we see the **Initial Setup** screen that we saw in *Chapter 2, Installing and Running Hudson*. Leave the defaults and click on the **Finish** button at the bottom of the page. After Hudson performs an initial setup and configuration, the screen should look similar to the Hudson home screen that we have seen earlier. The primary difference is a Logger Console section in the left part of the screen.

Creating a sample job

To see `sample-plugin` in action, we will create a sample job. From the Hudson home page, click on the **New Job** link in the left panel. To match the plugin name, we will give our job the name: `Sample Job`. Leave the **Build a free-style software project** radio button selected. Then, click on the **OK** button.

The **New Job** screen is shown in the following screenshot:

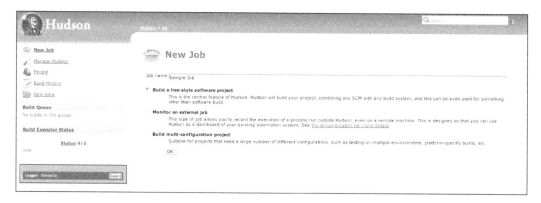

The **Job Configurations** page contains the definition of **Sample Job** that we have just created. On the **Job Configurations** page, we will add a build step by selecting the **Say hello world** option in the **Add build step** option. We will enter Hudson in the **Name** text box that appears. Then, click on the **Save** button at the bottom of the page. The **Job Configurations** screen is shown in the following screenshot:

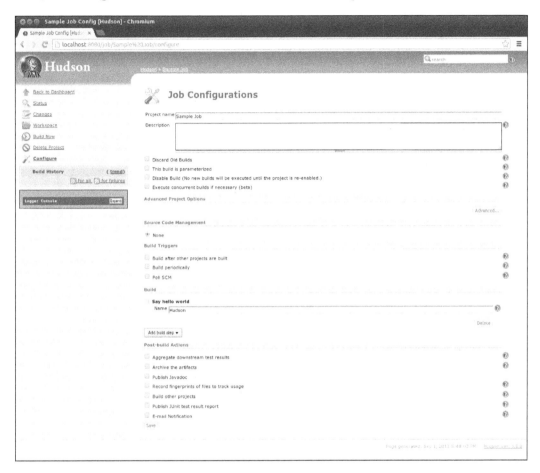

We are now on the **Project Sample Job** page, which displays all information about **Sample Job** that we have just created. The screen should look similar to the following screenshot:

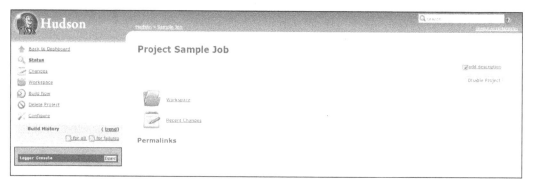

We will click on the **Build Now** link in the left column. We should see an entry appear in the **Build History** pane on the left-hand side of the page. Click on the **Latest Console output** link in the middle pane of the page, or click on the console icon in the **Build History** section. The **Console Output** screen is shown in the following screenshot:

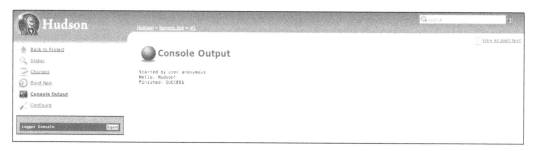

What happened?

The sample-plugin project has added an extension to the Hudson builder UI (the **Say hello world** build step). The plugin has provided a method to configure our extension (the **Name** text box). The plugin has also added a personalized message to the **Console Output** screen.

How did that happen?

The `HelloWorldBuilder.java` source code in our `sample-plugin` project contains much of the plugin's functionality. Hudson has a number of extension points. The builder class that our `HelloWorldBuilder` class extends is an extension point for the builder interface. The following simplified version of the `perform()` method implements the build step, which we can see is printing output to the logger:

```
@Override
public boolean perform(AbstractBuild build, Launcher launcher,
BuildListener listener) {
    listener.getLogger().println("Hello, "+name+"!");
    return true;
}
```

The `HelloWorldBuilder` class also contains the method that generates the text that is displayed in the **Add build step** menu in the **Job Configurations** screen:

```
public String getDisplayName() {
    return "Say hello world";
}
```

The `config.jelly` file contains the local configuration for the extension that `HelloWorldBuilder` is implementing. The simplified `config.jelly` code is:

```
<j:jelly xmlns:j="jelly:core" xmlns:st="jelly:stapler"
  xmlns:d="jelly:define" xmlns:l="/lib/layout"
    xmlns:t="/lib/hudson" xmlns:f="/lib/form">
  <f:entry title="Name" field="name">
    <f:textbox />
  </f:entry>
</j:jelly>
```

The `f:entry` tag tells Hudson that the enclosed tags are the UI elements that are submitted via an HTML form, which is a textbox in our case. The title value of the `f:entry` tag is the text that is displayed next to the textbox. The field value of the `f:entry` tag is the variable name that stores the text value that is displayed/entered in the textbox. The field value of the `f:entry` tag is used for two purposes (by convention):

- To retrieve the value of the name variable by calling the `HelloWorldBuilder.getName()` method

- To load the contents of the `help-name.html` help text

What else can I do?

Hudson is designed to be extensible and covering all plugin development topics are beyond the scope of this book. More information can be found on the Hudson wiki at `http://wiki.eclipse.org/Hudson-ci/Extend_Hudson`.

Deploying sample-plugin to our Hudson installation

The HPI Maven plugin can also generate an HPI file. We can deploy this file to our standalone Hudson installation. In our `sample-plugin` directory, type the following command:

```
mvn package
```

This will create the file at `target/sample-plugin.hpi`.

Stop the development version of Hudson that we have been using to test Hudson by typing *Ctrl + C* in the terminal window in which you started Hudson. Change to the directory that contains the `hudson-3.0.1.war` file and start Hudson with the command:

```
java -jar hudson-3.0.1.war
```

In your web browser, go to the Hudson home page at `http://localhost:8080`.

On the Hudson home page, click on **Manage Hudson** in the left pane. On the **Manage Hudson** page, click on **Manage Plugins** in the center pane. On the **Hudson Plugin Manager** page, select the **Advanced** tab in the center pane. The screen is shown in the following screenshot:

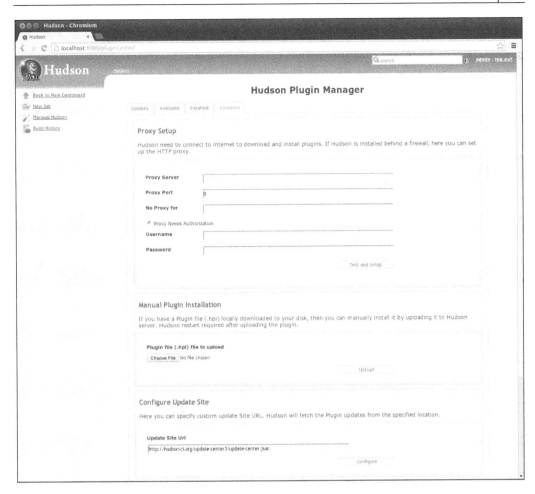

In the **Manual Plugin Installation** panel of the main panel, click on the **Choose File** button, select the `sample-plugin.hpi` file that we have just created, and click on the **Upload** button. Hudson must be restarted for the plugin to be available.

You can now create a sample job as we did and verify that the plugin is working as expected.

The sample-plugin project source code on Github

The source code for the `sample-plugin` project is available on Github at:
`https://github.com/javabilities/sample-plugin`

Summary

In this chapter, we have described the Hudson plugin system and installed some common plugins. We have defined and configured a backup strategy using the ThinBackup plugin. We have also seen how to create our own plugin project, how to test it in the development mode, and to deploy it to our standalone Hudson instance. In the next chapter, we will begin using this knowledge to configure, build, and deploy jobs.

5
Building and Delivering with Hudson

This chapter is about using Hudson to create jobs that can build and/or deploy applications. These jobs can be scheduled or initiated manually. Some builds may be automatically deployed on change to a version control system or scheduled build, and other builds may be deployed in a more controlled manner.

Using Maven to build a sample project

We will use a sample project from the open source Spring Framework project called `spring-petclinic`. This project is built with the Maven build tool.

> Information about **Spring Framework** can be found at
> `http://projects.spring.io/spring-framework/`.
> Information about the **Pet Clinic** demonstration project can be
> found at `http://docs.spring.io/docs/petclinic.html`.
> Information about **Maven** can be found at
> `http://maven.apache.org/`.

Creating a free-style software job for the Maven job

We will create a free-style software job by clicking on the **New Job** link on the left pane of the **Hudson** home page. The value for **Job name** is `spring-petclinic`. The screenshot is shown as follows:

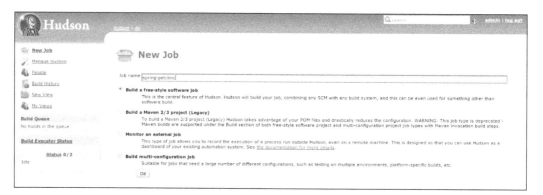

Click on the **OK** button at the bottom of the page. After clicking on the **OK** button, you will be taken to the **Job Configurations** page. Some of the options on this page are enabled by default, and some of the options are enabled by the plugins that have been installed.

Configuring Source Code Management for the Maven job

In the **Source Code Management** section of the **Job Configurations** page, select **Git** (we installed the Git plugin in *Chapter 4, Installing and Developing Hudson Plugins*). In the **URL of repository** section, enter the Github location of the `spring-petclinic` application, that is, `https://github.com/spring-projects/spring-petclinic.git`.

Your screen should look similar to the following screenshot:

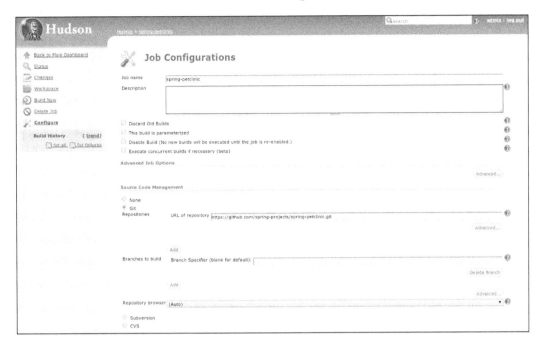

Configuring the build step for the Maven job

The `spring-petclinic` application is built with Maven. In the **Build** section of the
Job Configurations page, select the **Invoke Maven 3** option in the **Add build step**
drop-down menu. Leave the default values for all of the fields. The **Build** section
of the page should look as follows:

The **Maven 3** field determines which Maven installation should be used. Maven
is included with a Hudson installation and that can be used by leaving the default
(Bundled) option selected.

The **Goals** field specifies which Maven build phase (goal) will be executed.

 More information about the Maven build phases can be found at `http://maven.apache.org/guides/introduction/introduction-to-the-lifecycle.html`.

We will leave the default build phase selected, which is `clean install`; `clean` will remove all files generated by a previous build and `install` will install the package (the WAR file) into the local repository and allow it to be used as a dependency in other local projects.

The **Properties** field specifies custom properties that will be passed to Maven. The `spring-petclinic` build doesn't require any custom properties, so we will leave it blank.

The **Advanced** button will display other fields that can be used to customize the Maven job. It is a good idea to look at them. Click on the question mark icon to get an idea of which Maven settings can be controlled from the Hudson job.

Saving the Maven job

Click on the **Save** button at the bottom of the page. We should now be on the **Hudson** job page for `spring-petclinic`, which is shown as follows:

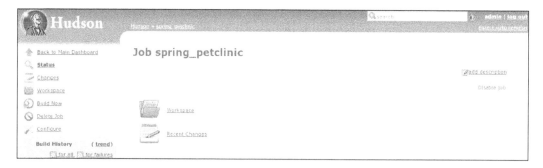

Manually building the Maven job

Click on the **Build Now** button in the left navigation column. There will be an entry in the **Build History** box at the bottom of the left navigation column. Click on the console icon (shown as follows) to see the progress or result of the build:

After the job has completed, there will be either a green ball (on success) or a red ball (on failure) to the left of the build in the **Build History** box. It should look as follows:

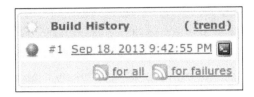

There are also two RSS icons for adding a feed for all the builds, or for failed builds, to your RSS reader.

Clicking on the console icon in the **Build History** box will display the output of the job (the output from checking the project out of Github, and the output of the Maven build step).

We can verify whether the build has completed successfully or not, by checking for a green ball that appears in the **Build History** box next to the build. We can also verify whether the build has completed successfully from the **Hudson** home page, which shows the **Jobs Status** page showing the status for all the defined jobs.

The Hudson home directory structure

Internally, Hudson has created a directory for our job, downloaded the source code to the project, and built the project. The project is located in `${HOME}/.hudson/jobs/spring-petclinic`. This directory contains the XML representation of the project, the `config.xml` file.

The `${HOME}/.hudson/jobs/spring-petclinic/workspace` directory contains the source code that was checked out from Github. When Maven builds the project, a directory named `target` is created in the workspace directory. The `target` directory is the working directory for Maven and contains all of the compiled files and the build artifact, `petclinic.war`.

The `${HOME}/.hudson/jobs/spring-petclinic/builds` directory contains the result of the Hudson build, including the log file (the contents of the log file are displayed in the console icon in the Hudson application).

Using Gradle to build a sample project

Gradle is another open source tool used for building applications. Gradle provides the option for a project to create a wrapper. **Gradle Wrapper** is a script that will download and use the version of Gradle that the project was designed to be built with, which saves the effort of downloading, installing, and configuring Gradle yourself.

Gradle is built using Gradle (of course!). So, let's create a job that builds Gradle from the latest source.

 Information about Gradle can be found at the project's home page at http://www.gradle.org/.

Creating a free-style software job for the Gradle job

We will create a free-style software job, as we described in the *Creating a free-style software job for the Maven job* section, except that the job name will be Gradle.

Configuring Source Code Management for the Gradle job

We will configure the **Source Code Management** section to use Git as we did in the preceding section. In the **Source Code Management** section of the **Job Configurations** page, select **Git** (we installed the Git plugin in *Chapter 4, Installing and Developing Hudson Plugins*). In the **URL of repository** section, enter the Github location of the spring-petclinic application, that is, https://github.com/gradle/gradle.git.

Configure a build step for the Gradle job. In the **Build** section of the **Job Configurations** page, select the **Invoke Gradle script** option in the **Add build step** drop-down menu. Keep the default values for all of the fields.

The **Build** section of the page is shown as follows:

We will use Gradle Wrapper to perform the build.

Saving the Gradle job

Save the job as we did in the *Saving the Maven job* section.

Manually building the Gradle job

Manually build the job as we did in the *Manually building the Maven job* section.

We can verify whether the build has completed successfully or not by checking for a green ball that appears in **Build History** next to the build. We can also verify whether the build has completed successfully or not from the **Hudson** home page, which shows the **Jobs Status** page that has the status for all of the defined jobs.

We can verify that the Gradle distribution was built by checking the ${HOME} hudson/jobs/gradle/workspace/build/distributions directory that contains the Gradle all, bin and src distributions.

Using Grails to build a sample project

Grails is a full-stack framework for creating Java web applications. The term full-stack framework means that all of the components that are required to build a modern Java web application are included in the framework: a build system, a data access layer, an MVC framework, a view technology, and other components. Grails uses the Groovy JVM language to build a development and deployment environment that leverages proven Java technologies such as the Spring Framework, Hibernate, SiteMesh, and Quartz, to build a flexible and productive platform on which web applications can be built. The Grails platform also has a rich plugin system that allows the framework to be extended in many ways by the use of plugins. To demonstrate how a Grails application can be built with Hudson, we will build a popular plugin for integrating spring security into a Grails application: the **grails-spring-security-core** plugin.

Creating a free-style software job for the Grails job

We will create a free-style software job as we described earlier, except here the job's name is grails-spring-security-core.

Configuring Source Code Management for the Grails job

We will configure the Source Code Management section to use Git as we did in the *Configuring Source Code Management for the Gradle job* section.

In the **Source Code Management** section of the **Job Configurations** page, select **Git** (we installed the Git plugin in *Chapter 4, Installing and Developing Hudson Plugins*). In the URL of the repository, enter the Github location of the grails-spring-security-core plugin: `https://github.com/grails-plugins/ grails-spring-security-core.git`.

Installing the Grails Hudson 3 plugin

In order to build a Grails application, we must install the **Grails Hudson 3** plugin by following the directions from *Chapter 4, Installing and Developing Hudson Plugins*. From the **Hudson** home page, select the **Manage Hudson** link on the left navigation pane, then select the **Manage Plugins** link from the middle pane of the **Manage Hudson** page. From the **Hudson Plugin Manager** page, select the **Available** tab and the **Search** tab. Enter `grails` as **Search String** and click on the **Search** button.

The screenshot is shown as follows:

Click on the checkbox next to the **Grails plugin** option and click on the **Install** button at the bottom of the page. Hudson will need to be restarted for the plugin changes to take effect.

Downloading and configuring Grails

We need the Grails framework to build a Grails application. The Grails framework can be downloaded from `http://grails.org/download`. The grails-spring-security-core plugin should be built with Grails Version 2.0.4, which is not the latest version of Grails. On the download page, check the section named **Download previous release** and choose **2.0** in the **Select a major version** drop-down menu. In the **Grails 2.0 releases** grid, select the **Binary** link of the **2.0.4** release and save the file on your local file system. Unzip the downloaded file in the home directory of the Hudson user.

From the **Hudson** home page, select **Manage Hudson** from the left navigation pane and then select **Configure System** from the center pane. Find the **Grails** section in the center pane of the **System Configurations** screen and click on the **Add Grails** button. Enter `Grails 2.0.4` for **Grails Name**. Uncheck the **Install automatically** checkbox. Enter the Grails installation directory in the **Install directory** field.

The **Grails** section is shown as follows:

Then, click on the **Save** button at the bottom of the page.

Configuring the build step for the Grails job

From the **Hudson** home page, click on the grails-spring-security-plugin job
in the center pane of the screen. Click on **Configure**, on the left pane of the
grails-spring-security-plugin page. In the center pane of the **Job Configurations**
page, select **Build With Grails** from the **Add build step** menu. Select **Grails
2.0.4** in the **Grails Installation** field. In the **Targets** field, enter package-plugin.
This will create the plugin distribution file from the source code. The screenshot
of the build section is shown as follows:

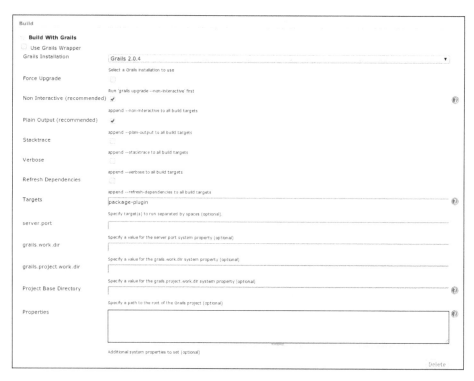

Saving the Grails job

Save the job as we did in the *Saving the Maven job* section.

Manually building the Grails job

Manually build the job as we did in the *Manually building the Maven job* section.

We can verify whether the build has completed successfully or not by checking for a green ball that appears in **Build History** next to the build. We can also verify whether the build has completed successfully from the **Hudson** home page, which shows the **Jobs Status** page showing the status for all the defined jobs.

We can verify that the Grails plugin was built by checking the ${HOME}/.hudson/jobs/grails-spring-security-plugin/workspace directory, which contains the grails-spring-security-core-1.2.7.3.zip Grails plugin file.

 The version number above (1.2.7.3) will almost certainly be different than what you will see from your job, since this project is very active and constantly improving and evolving.

Deploying a WAR file to an application server

Hudson 3 can also be used to deploy a WAR or EAR file to an application server. This can introduce the practice of continuous deployment in your IT organization. Continuous deployment is an aspect of **extreme programming** (**XP**) and is designed to improve the efficiency of software deployment.

Installing the Deploy to container Plugin and Copy Artifact Plugin

We will use two plugins to deploy our WAR file: **Deploy to container Plugin** and **Copy Artifact Plugin**. We will install these plugins by searching for them in the **Hudson Plugin Manager** screen and then installing them, as described in *Chapter 4, Installing and Developing Hudson Plugins*. From the **Hudson** home page, select the **Manage Hudson** link on the left navigation pane and then select the **Manage Plugins** link from the middle pane of the Manage Hudson page. From the **Hudson Plugin Manager** page, select the **Available** tab and the **Search** tab. Enter Deploy to container Plugin as **Search String**, and click on the **Search** button. Repeat the same for the "Copy Artifact Plugin". After the installation of these plugins, Hudson 3 will need to be restarted.

Reconfiguring Tomcat

In order to deploy the `spring-petclinic` WAR file to Tomcat, we need to make some configuration changes to the Tomcat application server that we installed and configured in *Chapter 2, Installing and Running Hudson.*

Stop the Tomcat server if it is running. Then, delete the `${TOMCAT_HOME}/webapps/hudson-3.0.1.war` file and the `${TOMCAT_HOME}/conf/Catalina/localhost/hudson.xml` file. This will undeploy the Hudson 3 web application.

Edit the `${TOMCAT_HOME}/conf/tomcat-users.xml` file, and add the following four lines of xml immediately before the `</tomcat-users>` tag:

```
<role rolename="manager-gui"/>

<role rolename="manager-script"/>

<user username="admin-gui" password="admin123" roles="manager-gui"/>

<user username="admin-script" password="admin123" roles="manager-script"/>
```

This will add the `admin-gui` user credentials that are used to view the Tomcat application server configuration and the `admin-script` user credentials that are used by the Deploy to container Plugin to install the WAR file to the Tomcat application server. Edit the `${TOMCAT_HOME}/conf/server.xml` file. Delete the following line:

```
<Connector port="8080" protocol="HTTP/1.1"
```

Insert the following line, in place of the preceding deleted line:

```
<Connector port="9090" protocol="HTTP/1.1"
```

This line comes somewhere around line 70 of the `server.xml` file.

This change configures the Tomcat application server to respond to HTTP requests on port `9090`, instead of the default port `8080`. This will allow our Hudson 3 application to remain available on port `8080` and our Tomcat application server to serve HTTP requests on port `9090`.

Now, start the Tomcat application server using the following command:

```
${TOMCAT_HOME}/bin/startup.sh
```

Verify whether Tomcat is running by viewing the default web page at `http://localhost:9090/`, and also the **Tomcat Web Application Manager** page at `http://localhost:9090/manager/html`.

Use the credentials we provided in the `tomcat-users.xml` file (username: `admin-gui` and password: `admin123`) to login to the **Tomcat Web Application Manager** page, shown as follows:

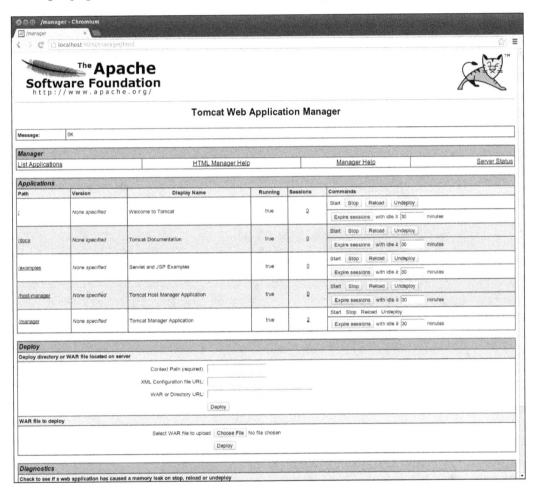

Configuring the Deploy build step

We will deploy the WAR file for the `spring-petclinic` project we created earlier to the Tomcat Application Server that we installed in *Chapter 2, Installing and Running Hudson*, and reconfigured in the previous section. This is accomplished by adding a post-build action to our `spring-petclinic` project. From the **Hudson** home screen in the **Jobs Status** pane, click on the `spring-petclinic` project. On the `spring-petclinic` job page, click on the **Configure** button present in the left navigation pane of the page. In the **Post-build Actions** section of the middle pane, check the **Deploy war/ear to a container** checkbox. Enter the following values for their respective fields in the **Deploy war/ear to a container** form that is now displayed:

- **WAR/EAR files**: `target/petclinic.war`
- **Context path**: We will use the Tomcat application servers default context path, so do not enter a value in the field
- **Container**: Tomcat 7.x
- **Manager user name**: `admin-script`
- **Manager password**: `admin123`
- **Tomcat URL**: `http://localhost:9090`

This section is shown in the following screenshot:

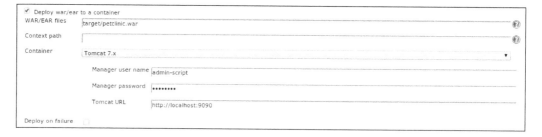

Click on the **Save** button at the bottom of the screen to save the job modifications.

Executing and validating the job

After saving the job modifications, we are on the `spring-petclinic` job. Click on the **Build Now** button in the left navigation column. Click on the console icon in the **Build History** box to watch the job as it is executing.

To verify whether the build completed correctly or not, the console should end with text similar to the following:

```
Deploying /home/meinholz/.hudson/jobs/spring-petclinic/workspace/target/
petclinic.war to container Tomcat 7.x Remote

  [/home/meinholz/.hudson/jobs/spring-petclinic/workspace/target/
petclinic.war] is not deployed. Doing a fresh deployment.

  Deploying [/home/meinholz/.hudson/jobs/spring-petclinic/workspace/
target/petclinic.war]

Finished: SUCCESS
```

We can verify that the Pet Clinic application is deployed properly by checking for an entry from it in the Tomcat Web Application Manager at `http://localhost:9090/manager/html`, and also for seeing an entry for the Pet Clinic web application.

Finally, we can verify whether the application was deployed correctly or not by accessing it at `http://localhost:9090/petclinic/`.

The Pet Clinic application that we have just deployed via Hudson 3 is shown in the following screenshot:

When the `spring-petclinic` job is run and the Pet Clinic web application is already deployed, the Deploy to container Plugin will first undeploy the old Pet Clinic web application, and then redeploy the newly built Pet Clinic web application.

Performing a custom action with a Groovy script

Sometimes a complicated build may need to perform an action that neither Hudson 3 nor a plugin supports. In these cases, we can write a custom script that will perform these actions. We will use the Groovy programming language to implement this custom functionality. Groovy is a dynamic language that runs on the JVM. Groovy is syntactically similar to Java but simplifies many aspects of Java programming and can also be used as a scripting language.

> More information can be found about Groovy at the project home page at `http://groovy.codehaus.org/`. There are also many online tutorials and books to learn more about Groovy.

Configuring Groovy

We must define a Groovy installation for Hudson 3 to execute the Groovy scripts. From the **Hudson** home page, click on the **Manage Hudson** link in the left navigation column, and then select **Configure System** from the center pane of the **Manage Hudson** page. In the center pane of the **System Configurations** page, find the **Groovy** section and click on the **Add Groovy** button. Enter Groovy 1.8.2 in the **Groovy name** field and leave the default values in the other fields. This section is shown as follows:

Click on the **Save** button at the bottom of the screen.

Adding a Groovy build step to the job

We will add a Groovy build step to the spring-petclinic job. From the **Hudson** home screen in the **Jobs Status** pane, click on the spring-petclinic project. On the spring-petclinic job page, click on the **Configure** button in the left navigation pane of the page. In the center pane of the **Job Configurations** page for the spring-petclinic job, look for the **Add build step** menu in the **Build** section of the page. Click on the **Add build step** menu and select **Execute system Groovy script**. The screenshot is shown as follows:

The **Execute Groovy script** option will fork a new JVM for the script to run in. The **Execute system Groovy Script** option will execute a Groovy script within the same JVM that Hudson 3 is running in. We want to use the system Groovy script in order to access Hudson's internals. This will give our script the access to the information about the current and previous builds and the Hudson settings.

 Since the system Groovy script has access to Hudson internals, a script may change or delete the Hudson configuration which could be a security risk.

Click on the **Groovy script file** radio button and enter ${HOME}/hudson/scripts/ testScript.groovy in the **Groovy script file** field.

The screenshot is shown as follows:

The **Groovy command** radio button will allow you to add the Groovy commands directly in to the build. The **Advanced...** section of the system Groovy script configuration can be used to specify the properties and class path settings. Finally, click on the **Save** button at the bottom of this page.

The testScript.groovy Groovy script

We will store our scripts in a directory outside the Hudson 3 home directory. Create the ${HOME}/hudson/scripts directory to store our Groovy scripts, and create the testScript.groovy file in that directory. The contents of the testScript.groovy file are:

```
import hudson.model.*


println "Test system Groovy scripting."


// Hashmap to store the configuration settings

def config = [:]


// Get the build settings from Hudson

def thread = Thread.currentThread()

def build = thread?.executable

config.putAll(build.parent.builds[0].properties.get("env Vars"))
```

```
println "Hudson Build Settings"

config.keySet().each { key ->

    println "  key(${key}) - value(${config.get(key)})"

}



// Create a temporary build directory

"mkdir -p /tmp/testScriptWork".execute()



// Copy the war file to the temporary build directory

def workspaceDir = config.WORKSPACE

def ant = new AntBuilder()

ant.copy(todir:"/tmp/testScriptWork") {

    fileset(dir:"${workspaceDir}/target") {

        include(name:"*.war")

    }

}
```

The script will get the build settings from Hudson and the environment variables and store them in `config` HashMap. The script will then iterate through each of these settings and print the key and the value to `stdout`. The output of the `println` statement will be displayed in the execution console output in Hudson. The script then demonstrates how to create a directory (this is OS specific) and then will copy the WAR file that we created in this new directory. Copying the file is accomplished by using Groovy's `AntBuilder` class which allows us to execute the Ant tasks in a Groovy builder-style markup.

We can execute the script by clicking on the **Build Now** link in the left navigation pane of the spring-petclinic page. After the job has completed, we can verify whether the output from the script was included in the Hudson output by clicking on the console icon next to the build that was just performed. There should be text towards the end of the console output similar to what is contained in the following screenshot:

```
Test system Groovy scripting.
Hudson Build Settings
  key(_) - value(/usr/java/bin/java)
  key(__array_start) - value(0)
  key(_first) - value(0)
  key(_second) - value(1)
  key(ADT_HOME) - value(/home/meinholz/ADT/android-sdk-linux)
  key(ANT_HOME) - value(/usr/local/apache/ant)
  key(ANT_OPTS) - value(-Xms512m -Xmx1024m)
  key(BUILD_ID) - value(2013-11-14_19-39-41)
  key(BUILD_NUMBER) - value(2)
  key(BUILD_TAG) - value(hudson-spring-petclinic-2)
  key(CLASSPATH) - value()
  key(COLORTERM) - value(gnome-terminal)
  key(COMPIZ_BIN_PATH) - value(/usr/bin/)
  key(COMPIZ_CONFIG_PROFILE) - value(ubuntu)
  key(DBUS_SESSION_BUS_ADDRESS) - value(unix:abstract=/tmp/dbus-fvWRZV1Qib,guid=141134492444f2af8593d6c7527ce58d)
  key(DEFAULTS_PATH) - value(/usr/share/gconf/ubuntu.default.path)
  key(DESKTOP_SESSION) - value(ubuntu)
  key(DISPLAY) - value(:0)
  key(EDITOR) - value(/usr/bin/vi)
  key(EDITOR) - value(/usr/bin/vi)
  key(ENV) - value(/home/meinholz/.profile)
  key(escape_flag) - value(1)
  key(EXECUTOR_NUMBER) - value(1)
  key(GDMSESSION) - value(ubuntu)
  key(GEM_HOME) - value(/home/meinholz/.rvm/gems/ruby-2.0.0-p0)
  key(GEM_PATH) - value(/home/meinholz/.rvm/gems/ruby-2.0.0-p0:/home/meinholz/.rvm/gems/ruby-2.0.0-p0@global)
  key(GIT_BRANCH) - value(master)
  key(GIT_COMMIT) - value(34d8ca46ac9add81362532e41461ceb52aa67fbc)
  key(GNOME_DESKTOP_SESSION_ID) - value(this-is-deprecated)
  key(GNOME_KEYRING_CONTROL) - value(/run/user/meinholz/keyring-bmNDwl)
  key(GNOME_KEYRING_PID) - value(2835)
  key(GPG_AGENT_INFO) - value(/run/user/meinholz/keyring-bmNDwl/gpg:0:1)
  key(GRADLE_HOME) - value(/usr/gradle)
  key(GRAILS_HOME) - value(/usr/grails)
  key(GROOVY_HOME) - value(/usr/groovy)
  key(GTK_MODULES) - value(overlay-scrollbar)
  key(GWT_HOME) - value(/home/meinholz/GWT/gwt-2.5.1)
  key(HOME) - value(/home/meinholz)
  key(HUDSON_HOME) - value(/home/meinholz/.hudson)
  key(HUDSON_SERVER_COOKIE) - value(cb741e5a4b1421bf23a39b7fb24cedb2)
  key(HUDSON_USER) - value(admin)
  key(IRBRC) - value(/home/meinholz/.rvm/rubies/ruby-2.0.0-p0/.irbrc)
  key(JAVA_HOME) - value(/usr/java)
  key(JBOSS_HOME) - value(/home/meinholz/Servers/EAP-6.1.0/jboss-eap-6.1)
  key(JOB_NAME) - value(spring-petclinic)
  key(JRUBY_HOME) - value(/usr/jruby)
  key(LANG) - value(en_US.UTF-8)
  key(LESSCLOSE) - value(/usr/bin/lesspipe %s %s)
  key(LESSOPEN) - value(| /usr/bin/lesspipe %s)
```

Finally, confirm that the petclinic.war file has been copied to the /tmp/testScriptWork directory. Hopefully, this short script has demonstrated some of the powerful capabilities that using Groovy can add to Hudson 3.

Summary

In this chapter, we have seen how Hudson 3 can be used for building and packaging diverse applications (a web application, a standalone application, and a Grails plugin) using different build technologies (Maven, Gradle and Grails). We have also seen how Hudson 3 can be used to deploy web applications to an application server. We have written a Groovy script that implements a custom build step for an example job. In the next chapter, we will see how Hudson 3 can help us maintain the code quality and generate project documentation.

6
Testing and Reporting with Hudson

This chapter describes the ways to use Hudson to execute tests and generate and view the test results. These jobs can be scheduled or initiated manually. Testing can be used to generate metrics that can provide insights into the health of a software project. These metrics can be generated from build tools such as Ant, Maven, and Gradle. However, the benefits of generating and storing these reports in Hudson is that they can be generated following a schedule, that they can be made available in a central location (Hudson) to all team members and that team members don't need to install and use a build tool in order to view the latest reports.

To begin our testing and reporting, we will create a new Hudson 3 job.

The hudsonDemoProject

The hudsonDemoProject application is a Java web application that is implemented using the Spring MVC Framework. The project is hosted on GitHub and uses Gradle as its build tool. Unlike the projects we have used previously, this is a toy application with very little functionality.

Creating a free-style software job

Create a free-style software job named hudsonDemoProject as we did in *Chapter 5, Building and Delivering with Hudson*. Click on the **New Job** link in the left-hand side panel of the Hudson home page. The job name is hudsonDemoProject.

The screen should look similar to the following screenshot:

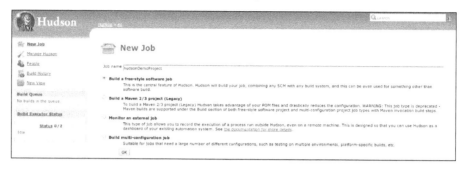

Click on the **OK** button at the bottom of the page. After clicking the **OK** button, you will be on the **Job Configurations** page. Some of the options on this page are enabled by default, and some of the options are enabled by plugins that have been installed.

Configuring Source Code Management

In the **Source Code Management** section of the **Job Configurations** page, select **Git** (we installed the **Git** plugin in *Chapter 4, Installing and Developing Hudson Plugins*. In the URL of the repository, enter the GitHub location of the hudsonDemoProject application:

```
https://github.com/javabilities/hudsonDemoProject.git
```

Your screen will look similar to the following screenshot:

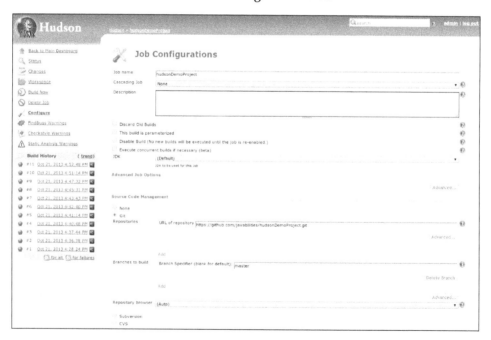

The project layout

The hudsonDemoProject uses Gradle to build the application. The application is a Java application and is implemented using the Spring MVC framework. Using the GitHub address for the project listed previously, you can download a ZIP distribution of the project to view the project source code. The layout of the project is similar to the following screenshot:

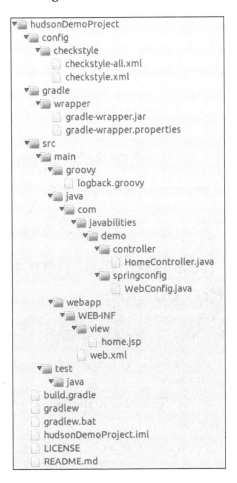

Generating and publishing Javadoc

In the next section, we will create our Javadoc by executing a Gradle task and then publish the Javadoc with a Hudson 3 post-build action.

Configure a build step in the **Build** section of the **Job Configurations** page, select the **Invoke Gradle script** option in the **Add build step** pull-down menu. Check the box next to **Use Gradle Wrapper** and leave the defaults for all the other fields. The **Build** section of the page should look similar to the following screenshot:

We will use the Gradle Wrapper to perform the build. The Gradle Wrapper is a script that will download and use the version of Gradle that the project was designed to be built with, which saves the effort of downloading and configuring Gradle yourself.

This `javadoc` task will create a Javadoc for the project.

Configuring a post-build action for the hudsonDemoProject job

The Javadoc task has now been created by the Gradle build script. To publish Javadoc on the project home page, we need to configure a post-build action.

1. In the **Post-build Actions** section of the **Job Configurations** page, check the box next to **Publish Javadoc**.

2. Enter the text `build/docs/javadoc` in the Javadoc directory text box.

3. Click on the **Save** button.

4. On the `hudsonDemoProject` home page, click on the **Build Now** button.

After the build has been completed, there should be a new button and link on the left-hand side navigation panel for Javadoc. The updated left-hand side navigation panel should look similar to the following screenshot:

Running and publishing JUnit test reports

In the following sections, we will use Gradle tasks that will execute projects tests and then publish the test results with a Hudson 3 post-build action.

Updating the Gradle build step for the hudsonDemoProject job

In the **Build** section of the **Job Configurations** page, update the **Tasks** in the **Invoke Gradle script** build step by adding the text `test` to the **Tasks** text box. The **Build** section of the page should look similar to the following screenshot:

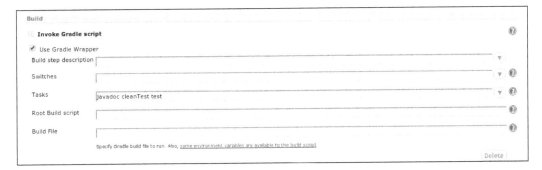

The `cleanTest` task is required to force Gradle to run the tests even if it isn't necessary. If this is not done, the Hudson job will fail as it believes the test results are outdated.

This build step will run the test for the project, which will generate test reports in the directory `build/test-results`.

Configuring a post-build action

The test results have now been created by the Gradle build script. To publish the test results on the project home page, we need to configure a post-build action.

1. In the **Post-build Actions** section of the **Job Configurations** page, check the box next to the **Publish JUnit** test result report.

2. Enter the text `build/test-results/*.xml` in the directory text box of the test report XML.

3. Click on the **Save** button.

4. On the `hudsonDemoProject` home page, click on the **Build Now** button.

5. After the job has been completed, click on the **Build Now** button again so that Hudson 3 can generate the trend graph.

After the job has been completed for the second time, there should be a new button and link on the center content panel for the latest test results, as well as a **Test Result Trend** graph. The center content panel should look similar to the following screenshot:

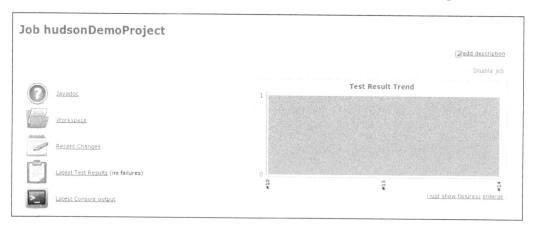

You can click on the **Latest Test Results** link and view the tests that have been run and determine which ones, if any, have failed.

Static source code analysis

The Static Analysis Collector plugin that we installed in *Chapter 4*, *Installing and Developing Hudson* Plugins, provides the following plugins:

- Checkstyle plugin
- DRY plugin
- FindBugs plugin
- PMD plugin
- Compiler Warnings plugin
- Task Scanner plugin

Static code analysis can be performed on a source code that is not being executed. This analysis can be used to find coding errors and security bugs, as well as to verify that the source code is written following a specific style. Using the output of this analysis can help developers catch problems before the application is tested and can give some assurance that the specified coding standards are being followed.

PMD

PMD is a source code analyzer that will find common defects. It supports a number of languages including Java. PMD analysis will find bugs, if any, as well as suboptimal, overly complex, dead, or duplicate code. More information about PMD can be found at the project home page `http://pmd.sourceforge.net/`.

FindBugs

FindBugs is a Java code analyzer that looks for bugs in Java class files, rather than the Java source code. More information about FindBugs can be found at the project home page `http://findbugs.sourceforge.net/`.

Checkstyle

Checkstyle is a tool that analyzes the source code and determines whether or not the code follows a specified set of standards, for example, the Sun Code Conventions: `http://www.oracle.com/technetwork/java/codeconv-138413.html`

More information about Checkstyle can be found at the project home page `http://checkstyle.sourceforge.net/`.

More about the Gradle build file

The Gradle build file is `build.gradle`. Like Hudson 3, Gradle also has a plugin system and functionality that can be added to a build through the use of a plugin. In order for the static analysis plugins to work, the build, whether the project is using Ant, Maven, or Gradle, needs to generate the PMD, FindBugs, and Checkstyle analysis results (or reports). Each of the projects (PMD, FindBugs, and Checkstyle) offers methods to integrate with each of the build tools. We accomplish this with Gradle by installing the appropriate plugins in the `build.gradle` file as follows:

```
apply plugin: 'checkstyle'
apply plugin: 'findbugs'
apply plugin: 'pmd'
```

The `checkstyle` plugin requires a configuration file that specifies which Checkstyle rules to use when evaluating the application. This configuration file is in the `hudsonDemoProject` directory:

```
config/checkstyle/checkstyle.xml
```

The Gradle task will create the following reports' files in the `hudsonDemoProject` directory:

```
build/reports/checkstyle/main.xml
build/reports/findbugs/main.xml
build/reports/pmd/main.xml
```

The location of these reports is needed for configuration of the Hudson 3 job.

The following file specifies the Checkstyle rules to be used:

```
config/checkstyle/checkstyle.xml
```

See the Checkstyle project home page mentioned previously, for more details on rules that are available and ways to create custom rules.

The PMD rulesets to be used are specified in the `build.gradle` file in the PMD section. See the PMD project home page mentioned earlier for more details on the rulesets that are available and the ways to create custom rulesets.

Updating the Gradle build step

The `hudsonDemoProject` is built with Gradle. In the **Build** section of the **Job Configurations** page, select the **Invoke Gradle script** option in the **Add build step** pull-down menu. Leave the defaults for all the fields.

In the **Build** section of the **Job Configurations** page, update the **Tasks** textbox in the **Invoke Gradle script** build step by adding the text `checkstyleMain findbugsMain pmdMain war` to the **Tasks** textbox. The **Build** section of the page should look similar to the following screenshot:

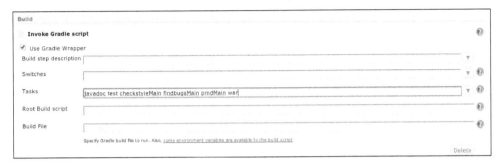

The tasks executed by the build step will run the Checkstyle plugin, the FindBugs plugin, the PMD plugin, and then build the WAR file for the project.

Configuring post-build actions for the hudsonDemoProject job

The reports for the static analysis tools (PMD, FindBugs and Checkstyle) will be built by the Gradle plugins and tasks. Now, to include the reports' analysis in Hudson 3, we need to configure some post-build actions.

In the **Post-build Actions** section of the **Job Configurations** page, check the box next to:

- **Publish PMD analysis results**
- **Publish FindBugs analysis results**
- **Publish Checkstyle analysis results**
- **Publish combined analysis results**

Enter the following text in the PMD results text box:

`build/reports/pmd/main.xml`

Enter the following text in the FindBugs results text box:

`build/reports/findbugs/main.xml`

Enter the following text in the Checkstyle results text box:

`build/reports/checkstyle/main.xml`

These are the files that the Gradle build has created.

Click on the checkbox next to each of the warnings in the **Publish combined analysis results** section.

The **Post-build Actions** section should look similar to the following:

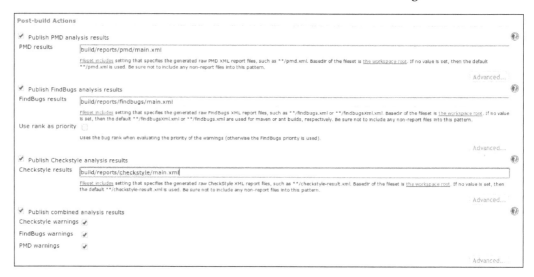

Click on the **Save** button.

Building and analyzing the results for the hudsonDemoProject

On the `hudsonDemoProject` home page, click on the **Build Now** button in the left-hand side navigation panel. After the build has been completed, you should notice new entries in the left-hand side navigation panel for **PMD Warnings**, **FindBugs Warnings**, **Checkstyle Warnings**, and **Static Analysis Warnings**. The left-hand side navigation panel will look similar to the following screenshot:

Each of these sections has details about the categories or types of warnings, the files in which they occurred, and even the section of code that has generated the warning. These warnings are prioritized as high, normal and low priority. These sections will also keep a total of **All Warnings**, **New Warnings**, and **Fixed Warnings**, which is useful for determining progress in addressing these issues. An example of this is the **PMD Result** screen, which can be viewed by clicking on the **PMD Warnings** link on the left-hand side navigation panel. The screen should look similar to the following screenshot:

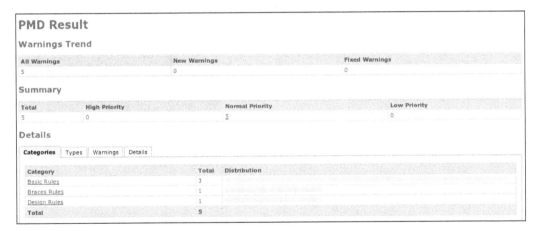

Trend analysis of hudsonDemoProject

In order to see a trend, we need to execute another build. On the hudsonDemoProject home page, click on the **Build Now** button in the left-hand side navigation panel. After the job has been completed, we should see trend graphs in the main panel of the hudsonDemoProject home page. The page should look similar to the following screenshot:

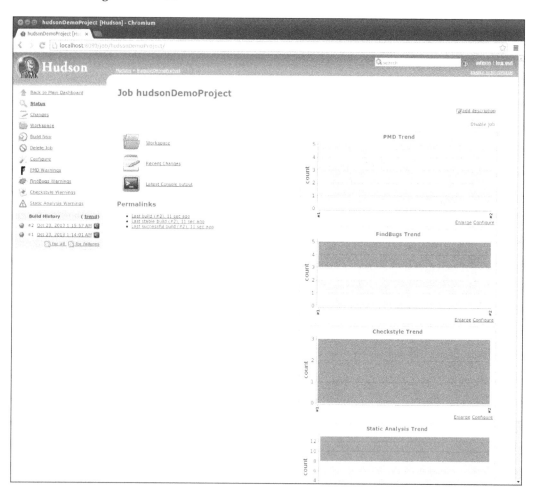

The graph is not very interesting, since the `hudsonDemoProject` has very few lines of code and warnings, but this analysis can provide a quick insight into the project's health over time.

Each of the graphs has an **Enlarge** link and a **Configure** link at the bottom right of the graph container. The **Enlarge** link allows a team member to get a closer look at the warnings and see the details. The **Configure** link allows a team member to resize the graph, set the number of builds and days that are included in the graph, and determine the types of graph and data that will be displayed.

Summary

In this chapter, we have seen the ways to use Hudson 3 to generate test reports and evaluate test coverage. We have used Hudson 3 to generate and publish Javadoc for our project. We have also seen how to use static code analysis tools to look for possible defects in our source code and generate reports to help interpret these results. In the next chapter, we will see different strategies to upgrade Hudson 3 and look at some of the new features that have been introduced in Hudson 3.1.

7
Upgrading Hudson and the Team Concept feature

This chapter will cover approaches to upgrade Hudson to a new version and also Team Concept, which is a new feature introduced in Hudson 3.1. Team Concept was developed and released while this book was being written.

Checking Hudson and plugin upgrade availability

New versions of Hudson are released often, and announcements are made on the old Hudson CI website at `http://hudson-ci.org`, as well as the new Hudson home on the eclipse website at `http://www.eclipse.org/hudson`.

An easier way of determining that a new release of Hudson is available is by looking on the **Manage Hudson** page for an alert in yellow at the top of the main panel, that looks similar to the following screenshot:

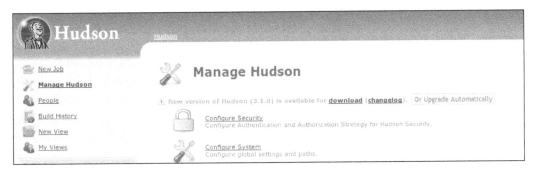

There may be two options for upgrading our Hudson installation

- Download a new WAR file
- Upgrading Hudson and the Team Concept feature

In some circumstances, the **Upgrade Automatically** option will not be available.

While upgrading Hudson to a new release, it is possible that there may be issues with plugin compatibility or something may go wrong during the upgrade process. For this reason, it is suggested that a full backup of the Hudson configuration is done before you perform an upgrade.

Backing up Hudson

We can manually trigger a full backup using the ThinBackup plugin that we installed in *Chapter 4, Installing and Developing Hudson Plugins*. To accomplish this, from the Hudson home page, click on the **Manage Hudson** link in the left navigation pane and then click on the **ThinBackup** link in the main page of the **Manage Hudson** page. On the **ThinBackup** page, click on the **Backup Now** button. After the backup has completed, verify that the backup exists by clicking on the **Restore** button and verifying that a backup with the correct timestamp exists in the restore backup from options. The page should look similar to the following screenshot:

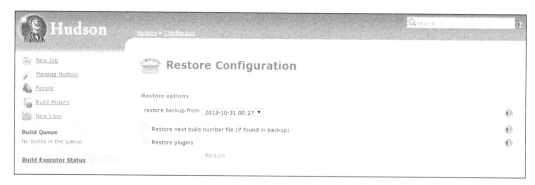

Other methods of backing up the Hudson configuration are to copy the entire `${HOME}/.hudson` directory to another location or to create an archive of the `${HOME}/.hudson` directory using TAR and GZIP on Unix-based platforms and 7-Zip on Windows-based installations. Copying the entire `.hudson` directory may not be practical if the `.hudson` directory is too large, making the archiving method a better choice. If either of these approaches is used, it is important to shut down Hudson before the directory is copied to prevent damage to files that may be in use.

Upgrading Hudson automatically

Clicking on **Upgrade Automatically** on the **Manage Hudson** page will create a backup of the current Hudson WAR file, download the new Hudson release, and install it. Hudson will have to be restarted for the new version of Hudson to be available.

This method of upgrading Hudson may not be available in all configurations. For example, if we are running Hudson from the WAR file, we need to have the new WAR file available and run it instead of the older version.

Installing a new standalone Hudson WAR file

This is the easiest scenario to upgrade Hudson. Download the latest Hudson WAR file from the **Download** link on the **Manage Hudson** page. Save the new WAR file to the same location as the older version of Hudson. Run the WAR file as we did in *Chapter 2, Installing and Running Hudson*, using the file name `java -jar hudson-3.1.0.war`.

Installing a new Hudson WAR file on Tomcat

To update the Hudson WAR file on the Tomcat configuration we described in *Chapter 2, Installing and Running Hudson*, perform the following steps:

1. Stop the Tomcat instance.
2. Modify `${TOMCAT_HOME}/conf/Catalina/localhost/hudson.xml` by changing `docBase="/home/meinholz/hudson/hudson-3.0.1.war"` to `docBase="/home/meinholz/hudson/hudson-3.1.0.war"`.
3. Start the Tomcat instance.

Installing a new Hudson WAR file on JBoss AS 7

On the JBoss AS 7 **Management Console** page, perform the following steps:

1. Select the **Manage Deployments** link in the left column.
2. Select the row for the hudson-3.0.1.war file in the **Deployments** pane.
3. Click on the **Remove** button.
4. Click on the **Confirm** button to confirm that we want to remove the WAR file from the Server.

5. Your screen should look similar to the following screenshot:

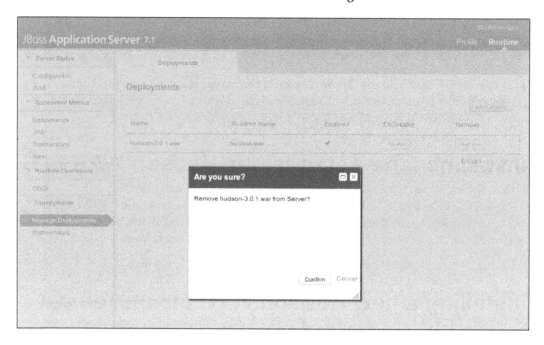

Deploy the `hudson-3.1.0.war` application to our JBoss AS 7 server, as we described in *Chapter 2, Installing and Running Hudson*.

Installing a new Hudson WAR file on GlassFish 4

On the GlassFish 4 Console page, perform the following steps:

1. Click on the **List Deployed Applications** tab in the Deployment section of the main panel.

2. Select the checkbox next to the hudson-3.0.1 application in the main panel.

3. Click on the **Undeploy** button in the main panel and then on **OK** on the confirmation pop-up.

4. Your screen should look similar to the following screenshot:

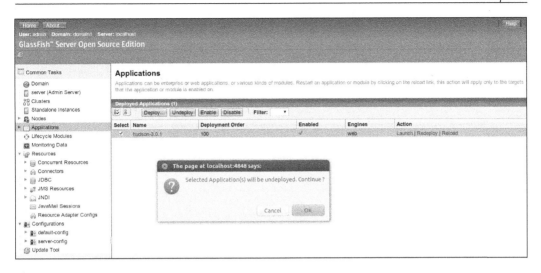

Deploy the `hudson-3.1.0.war` application to our GlassFish 4 server, as we described in *Chapter 2*, *Installing and Running Hudson*.

Team Concept

Team Concept is a new feature of Hudson 3.1. This feature adds role-based authorization to Hudson, which will allow multiple teams to work on a single instance of Hudson and not interfere with each other's jobs. To accomplish this with previous releases of Hudson, a separate instance of Hudson will have to be installed for each team or a complicated job-based Matrix Authorization Strategy will have to be configured and maintained.

Creating new users

We will create two teams of three users each. We will first create the users and then later assign them to teams.

From the Hudson home page, click on the **Manage Hudson** link in the left navigation column and then the **Manage Users** link from the main pane of the **Manage Hudson** screen. Click on the **Create User** link from the left navigation pane to create a user.

Create an account for each of the following users:

Username	Password	Full name	E-mail address
steve	avengers	Steve Rogers	`steve@localhost`
tony	avengers	Tony Stark	`tony@localhost`
bruce	avengers	Bruce Banner	`bruce@localhost`
xavier	xmen	Professor Xavier	`xavier@localhost`
scott	xmen	Scott Summers	`scott@localhost`
logan	xmen	Logan	`local@localhost`

After you have created all the users, the **Manage Users** link should look similar to the following screenshot:

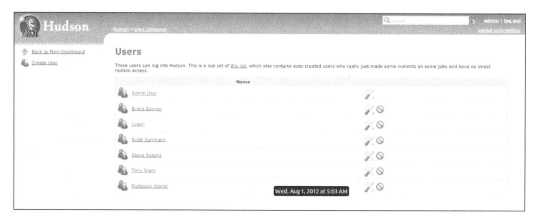

Configuring team-based authorization

At the end of *Chapter 3, Configuring and Securing Hudson,* we had configured our Hudson instance to use Hudson's internal user database and Matrix-based security. Our configuration had defined an admin user who had all privileges to our Hudson instance and anonymous users (users who were not logged in) who have read-only privileges to our Hudson instance. We will modify our configuration to use a team-based authorization strategy instead.

From the Hudson home page, click on the **Manage Hudson** link in the left navigation column and then the **Configure Security** link from the main pane of the **Manage Hudson** screen. In the **Authorization** section of the main page of the **Configure Security** page, change the authorization strategy from **Matrix-based security** to **Team based Authorization Strategy**. Your screen should look similar to the following screenshot:

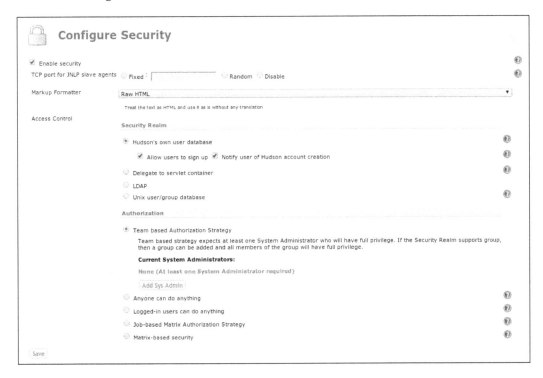

Using **Team based Authorization Strategy** requires that there be at least one System Administrator, so we will use our existing admin user. Click on the **Add Sys Admin** button and enter `admin` in the **User or Group Name** pop-up window.

By configuring team-based authorization, we have added a new entry to the left navigation page, that is, **Manage Teams**.

Creating teams

When we log in as any of the newly created users, we will not have any privileges and will not able to create or modify jobs.

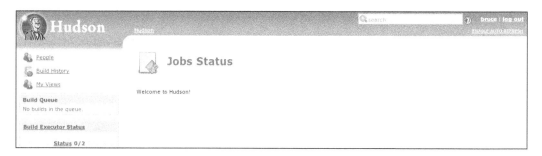

Log in as the admin user and click on the **Manage Teams** link from the left navigation pane. A warning that reads Hudson does not have any teams defined is displayed on the main page. From the **Manage Teams** tab in the center of the page, click on the **Add New Team** button. Enter the text Avengers and leave the other fields blank. The screen should look similar to the following screenshot:

Create another group named XMen.

If the **Name** field is **Avengers** and the **Custom team folder** is empty, the directory that will contain the team's jobs will be created in the `${HOME}/.hudson/teams/` `Avengers` directory. By keeping team configuration and team job definition in this folder, it is possible to specify that the team folder is on a different file system and that team working directories stay separated from each other.

Adding members to teams

Now we will add members to teams. On the **Manage Teams** page, select **Avengers** in the teams section and click on **Add New Member** in the members section. Your screen should look similar to the following screenshot:

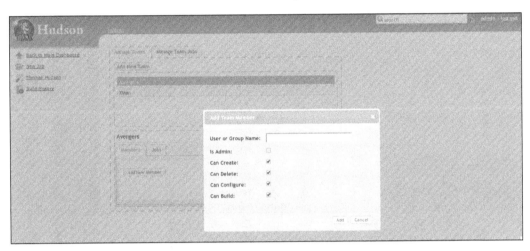

Enter `steve` in the **User or Group Name** field and leave the default values for the other options and click on the **Add** button. Also add `tony` and `bruce` to the **Avengers** team. The value of the username field is used for adding users but not the full name.

If you add a valid user by entering a value that is a username, a person icon will appear to the left of the user.

If you add an invalid user by entering a value that is not a username, a red icon will appear to the left of the user that implies do not enter.

An example of valid and invalid users is shown in the following screenshot:

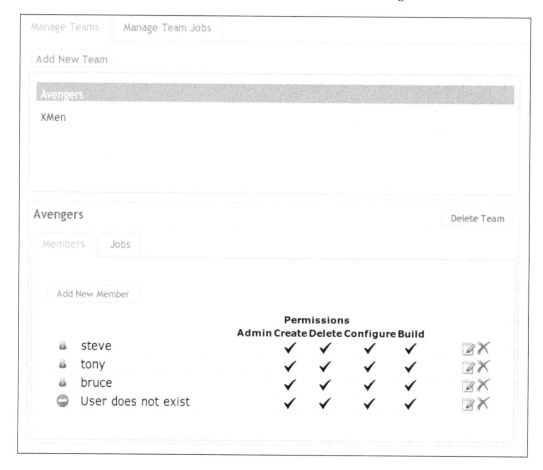

Creating new jobs

We will create three new jobs. One will be a job available to all users, one will be a job for the Avengers team, and one will be a job for the XMen team.

From the Hudson home page, click on the **New Job** link on the left navigation pane. Create a freestyle software job with the job name `Public Job`. Create two more jobs, one with the job name `Save New York` and the other with the job name `Capture Magneto`.

You can verify as any of the users or as the anonymous user (not logged in) whether all three jobs are visible on the Hudson home page.

Assigning jobs to teams

We want the **Save New York** job to only be visible by the Avengers team and the **Capture Magneto** job to only be visible by the XMen team.

Log in to Hudson as the admin user and click on the **Manage Teams** link on the left navigation pane. Click on the **Manage Team** Jobs tab in the main pane of the **Manage Teams** link. Click on the **Select** checkbox for the **Capture Magneto** job and click on the **Move Jobs** button. In the pop-up window, select **XMen** in the pull-down menu for the teams. Your screen should look similar to the following screenshot:

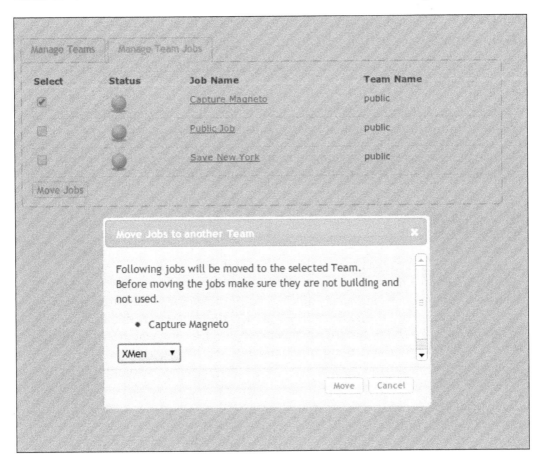

Similarly, select the **Save New York** job and move it to the Avengers team.

Navigate to the **Hudson Main Dashboard** by clicking on the Hudson logo in the upper-right region of the screen or by clicking on the **Back to Main Dashboard** link in the left navigation page. The name of the **Save New York** job has changed to **Avengers.Save New York** and the name of the **Capture Magneto** job has changed to **XMen.Capture Magneto**. This format (TEAM_NAME.JOB_NAME) signifies that the job belongs to a team, and is not a public job.

 The job names do not update in the **Manage Team Jobs** tab. Navigate to the Hudson home page to see the change in job name.

Verifying job visibility

When logging in as the admin user, all jobs are visible from the **Hudson Main Dashboard**.

When logging out and viewing the **Hudson Main Dashboard** as an anonymous user, only **Public Job** is visible.

When logging in as an Avengers team member, only the **Avengers.Save New York** and **Public Job** are visible from the **Hudson Main Dashboard**.

When logging in as an XMen team member, only the **Xmen.Capture Magneto** and **Public Job** are visible from the **Hudson Main Dashboard**.

Summary

We began this chapter by discussing different methods to backup and then upgrade our Hudson 3 installation. This is a task that we will almost certainly need to do in the future as new and improved versions of Hudson are released. We then configured a team-based authorization strategy for our Hudson instance and configured several team jobs. This is a new feature that was added in Hudson 3.1, which adds the ability for multiple teams to use the same instance of Hudson and still have their work isolated from each other.

Online Resources

Software downloads

Oracle JDK or OpenJDK can be used when running Hudson. It is easier to use the Oracle JDK on Windows or Mac OSX computers. Either Oracle JDK or OpenJDK are simple to use and install on Linux computers.

The location to download the Oracle JDK is:

```
http://www.oracle.com/technetwork/java/javase/downloads/index.html
```

The instructions for downloading and installing OpenJDK distribution on Linux are at the following location:

```
http://openjdk.java.net/install/index.html
```

The location to download the Hudson distribution is:

```
http://www.eclipse.org/hudson/download.php
```

Hudson resources

The Hudson home page is located at:

```
http://hudson-ci.org/
```

The Hudson page for the eclipse project is located at:

```
http://www.eclipse.org/hudson/
```

The Hudson Bugzilla site is located at:

```
https://bugs.eclipse.org/bugs/buglist.cgi?query_format=advanced;
bug_status=UNCONFIRMED;bug_status=NEW;bug_status=ASSIGNED;bug_status=
REOPENED;product=Hudson;list_id=166514
```

The Hudson Support Forum is located at:

```
http://www.eclipse.org/forums/index.php/f/229/
```

The Hudson IRC Channel is located at:

```
irc://irc.freenode.net/#eclipse-hudson
```

Application server resources

The Apache Tomcat 7 is available for download at:

```
http://tomcat.apache.org/download-70.cgi
```

WildFly is the new name for the community edition of the JBoss Application Server. It's available for download at:

```
http://www.wildfly.org/download/
```

The GlassFish download site is located at:

```
https://glassfish.java.net/download.html
```

Hudson 3 Essentials book projects

The project page and source code for the plugin that was created in *Chapter 4, Installing and Developing Hudson Plugins*, is available on GitHub at:

```
https://github.com/javabilities/sample-plugin
```

The project page and source code for the project that was used in *Chapter 6, Testing and Reporting with Hudson*, is available on GitHub at:

```
https://github.com/javabilities/hudsonDemoProject
```

Index

Search button 63
simple security policy
  defining 33-35
software downloads
  Hudson distribution, URL 101
  Oracle JDK, URL 101
Source Code Management
  configuring, for Gradle job 58
  configuring, for Grails job 60
  configuring, for Maven job 54
Static Analysis Collector plugin
  Checkstyle plugin 81
  FindBugs plugin 81
  PMD plugin 81
System Configurations page, Hudson
  Ant, configuring 28, 29
  JDK, configuring 28
  Maven, configuring 29, 30

T

team-based authorization
  configuring 94, 95
Team Concept
  about 93
  jobs, assigning to teams 99, 100
  job visibility, verifying 100
  members, adding to teams 97
  new jobs, creating 98, 99
  new users, creating 93
  team-based authorization, configuring 94,
    95
  teams, creating 96, 97
teams
  creating 96, 97
  Jobs, assigning to 99, 100
  members, adding to 97
Test-driven Development 6
Test Result Trend graph 80

testScript.groovy Groovy script
  creating 70, 71
  executing 72
ThinBackup plugin
  about 40, 41
  Backup Now 41
  backup set 42
  backup strategy 42, 43
  differential backups 42
  full backups 42
  Restore 41
  Settings 41
  using, for Hudson backup 90
Tomcat
  Hudson, deploying to 14
  Hudson WAR file, installing on 91
  installation 12
  reconfiguring 64, 65
  server downloading 12
Tomcat is 7.0.42 12

U

Undeploy button 92
Unix/Linux installation 12

W

WAR file
  deploying 66
  deploying, Copy Artifact Plugin used 63
  deploying, Deploy to container Plugin used
    63
  deploying, to application server 63
  deploying, to Tomcat 64, 65
WildFly
  URL 102

Thank you for buying
Hudson 3 Essentials

About Packt Publishing

Packt, pronounced 'packed', published its first book "*Mastering phpMyAdmin for Effective MySQL Management*" in April 2004 and subsequently continued to specialize in publishing highly focused books on specific technologies and solutions.

Our books and publications share the experiences of your fellow IT professionals in adapting and customizing today's systems, applications, and frameworks. Our solution based books give you the knowledge and power to customize the software and technologies you're using to get the job done. Packt books are more specific and less general than the IT books you have seen in the past. Our unique business model allows us to bring you more focused information, giving you more of what you need to know, and less of what you don't.

Packt is a modern, yet unique publishing company, which focuses on producing quality, cutting-edge books for communities of developers, administrators, and newbies alike. For more information, please visit our website: www.packtpub.com.

About Packt Open Source

In 2010, Packt launched two new brands, Packt Open Source and Packt Enterprise, in order to continue its focus on specialization. This book is part of the Packt Open Source brand, home to books published on software built around Open Source licences, and offering information to anybody from advanced developers to budding web designers. The Open Source brand also runs Packt's Open Source Royalty Scheme, by which Packt gives a royalty to each Open Source project about whose software a book is sold.

Writing for Packt

We welcome all inquiries from people who are interested in authoring. Book proposals should be sent to author@packtpub.com. If your book idea is still at an early stage and you would like to discuss it first before writing a formal book proposal, contact us; one of our commissioning editors will get in touch with you.

We're not just looking for published authors; if you have strong technical skills but no writing experience, our experienced editors can help you develop a writing career, or simply get some additional reward for your expertise.

Application Testing with Capybara

ISBN: 978-1-78328-125-1   Paperback: 104 pages

Confidently implement automated tests for web applications using Capybara

1. Learn everything to become super productive with this highly acclaimed test automation library

2. Using some advanced features, turn yourself into a Capybara ninja!

3. Packed with practical examples and easy-to-follow sample mark-up and test code

Instant Testing with QUnit

ISBN: 978-1-78328-217-3   Paperback: 64 pages

Employ QUnit to increase your efficiency when testing JavaScript code

1. Learn something new in an Instant! A short, fast, focused guide delivering immediate results

2. Learn about cross-browser testing with QUnit

3. Learn how to use popular QUnit plugins and develop your own plugins

4. Hands-on examples on all the essential QUnit methods

Please check **www.PacktPub.com** for information on our titles

www.ingramcontent.com/pod-product-compliance
Lightning Source LLC
LaVergne TN
LVHW081346050326
832903LV00024B/1346